Their Blo   ...ld Cold

Adventures with
Reptiles and Amphibians

DATE			
		JUL ▪▪ 1992	
		APR '87]	

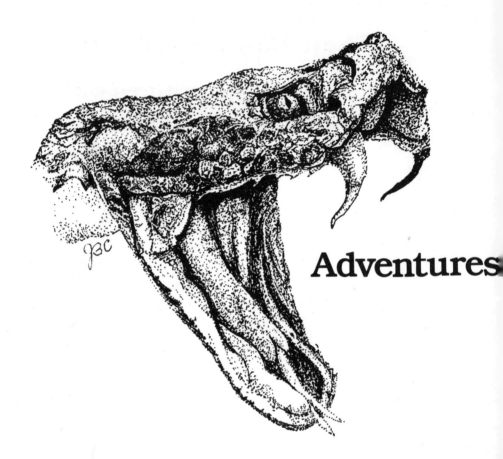

Adventures

Their Blood Runs Cold

with Reptiles and Amphibians

WHIT GIBBONS

THE UNIVERSITY OF ALABAMA PRESS

Copyright © 1983 by
The University of Alabama Press
University, Alabama 35486
Manufactured in the United States of America

SECOND PRINTING 1984

Library of Congress Cataloging in Publication Data

Gibbons, Whit, 1939–
   Their blood runs cold.

   Bibliography: p.
   Includes index.
   1. Reptiles.   2. Amphibians.   I. Title.
QL641.G5   1983   597.6   82-17395
ISBN 0-8173-0135-6
ISBN 0-8173-0133-X (pbk.)

For my mother,

Janie M. Gibbons

Contents

Foreword

Recently a group of students and faculty were discussing what it takes to be a successful scientist. Granting that innate talent and higher education are important, all agreed that enthusiasm for one's subject is an essential ingredient. If one enjoys delving deeply into some aspect of the world in which we live, that person will spend the extra hours and make the extra effort that is required for a successful career in science.

Because most people, including most scientists, have very little enthusiasm for reptiles and amphibians, herpetologists need to be genuinely infatuated with their subject if they are to attract attention to their work. Whit Gibbons is such a person. He is a dedicated naturalist and his enthusiasm is so contagious that in a very short time he can convince almost anyone that snakes and turtles and lizards are fascinating, if not downright lovable. Whit enjoys his work as a research scientist at the 190,000-acre Savannah River Plant, the Department of Energy's National Environmental Research Park where scientists seek solutions to difficult problems relating to energy development, and his enthusiasm is reflected in every page of this book. Paradoxically, the research park is also a wildlife paradise.

Whit also enjoys writing about his work and adventures in the field. The essays and stories assembled in this book are good reading and they contribute new insights into the ecology of a little known and much maligned group of animals.

Each of the eleven chapters reveals the exciting as well as the endearing qualities of reptiles and amphibians, taking into account not only how they are in real life but how we perceive them.

In the first chapter Whit analyzes the reasons why snakes and their kin are wrongly feared and loathed by many persons, or at least are considered insignificant in the human environmental scheme. A personal experience is related to show that ignorance, not only on the part of the layman but also by the medical doctor and the scientist, is an underlying cause of public misgivings and misunderstanding. The following chapters, one on each of the six major groups of reptiles and amphibians, include a series of true short stories, anecdotes, and fascinating facts that clearly drive home the message that none of us knows enough about these animals. The book tells us more than we have ever known about herpetology and makes us yearn to find out more.

Two of the chapters dwell on herpetological techniques of finding, catching, and studying these elusive and unusual animals. Not surprisingly, the methods are often unusual in themselves: X-ray photography to count turtle eggs, blowguns to catch lizards, and radioactive tags to find out where salamanders go in the summertime. Many of the techniques, now standard fare for the practicing field herpetologist, were developed on the Savannah River Plant and presented in technical journals by Whit and his colleagues at the Savannah River Ecology Laboratory.

The final two chapters give one cause for serious thought. Reptiles and amphibians are presented as an example of the conflicts that can arise in this nation and throughout the world as a result of ecological ignorance. Thus, Whit ends his book with the message that we will all be better off if we acquire a higher level of knowledge about snakes, turtles, lizards, salamanders, frogs, and alligators. And when you finish the book you will have done just that.

EUGENE P. ODUM

Acknowledgments

The indebtedness one has to others in undertaking a book is great. My utmost gratitude goes to my family—to my wife Carol for constant support and a rather unusual tolerance; to Laura, Jennifer, Susan Lane, and Michael for their special contributions; to my mother Janie, my father Bob, and my sister Anne and her husband Bill for their encouragement and editorial contributions; to my Aunt Harriet for suggesting I become a biologist, and to my mother and father for letting me.

My professional career was critically shaped by several scientists. The most influential of these was the late Dr. Donald W. Tinkle. Others include Drs. Ralph L. Chermock, Don L. McGregor, Joab L. Thomas, M. Max Hensley, George H. Lauff, John A. King, Gerald W. Esch, Richard G. Wiegert, Michael H. Smith, Frank B. Golley, Rebecca R. Sharitz, and Eugene P. Odum.

The threescore individuals who have worked with me as student or faculty research participants or technical assistants at the Savannah River Ecology Laboratory since 1967 have contributed in subtle and obvious ways. Special thanks go to Judith L. Greene, John W. Coker, David H. Nelson, Raymond D. Semlitsch, and David H. Bennett for their much-needed support during critical periods. I thank Rebecca R. Sharitz, Garfield H. Keaton, Joseph P. Schubauer, Janalee P. Caldwell, Stephen H. Bennett, Laurie J. Vitt, Justin D. Congdon, and Karen K. Patterson for reading parts of the manuscript. Dr. George R. Zug read the original version of the Selected References in Herpetology and suggested additional titles. Nancy Barber diligently typed the manuscript until it reached its final form. Jean Baldwin Coleman made the drawings labeled JBC.

I appreciate the encouragement of several individuals in nonbiological fields, including Joe Harris, Idella Bodie, Lynne Katonak, Isabelle Vandervelde, and other members of the Aiken Writers Group, as well as Don Law, Sam Cothran, and Bob Cathcart. I especially thank Janell Gregory for her help and encouragement.

I gratefully acknowledge the following for permission to modify magazine articles or newspaper columns for inclusion where appropriate: *Savannah River Plant News, Aiken Standard, South Carolina Wildlife* magazine, *EnviroSouth* magazine, *Sky* magazine, and *Augusta Spectator* magazine.

Article Credits

Parts or modifications of previously published articles have been used in some chapters. Those used from the January/March 1979, January/March 1980, April/June 1980, July/September 1980, October/December 1980, and the October/December 1981 issues of *EnviroSouth* magazine were reprinted with permission from EnviroSouth, Inc., P.O. Box 17111, Montgomery, AL 36117.

Material used from the Spring 1981 and Spring 1982 issues of the *Augusta Spectator* magazine were reprinted with permission from FKB Enterprises, Inc., Augusta, Georgia. *Sky* magazine, Halsey Publishing Company, Miami, Florida, gave permission to reprint parts of articles from April 1980, April 1981, April 1982, and July 1982. *South Carolina Wildlife* magazine, South Carolina Wildlife and Marine Resources Department, Columbia, South Carolina, gave permission to reprint parts of an article entitled "Who's Watching the Snakes?" from the March 1978 issue. *BioScience* magazine permitted the use of the cover photograph of the April 1981 issue to be used in this book.

Photo Credits

The photographs used in this book were taken by various individuals at the Savannah River Ecology Laboratory. Although some of the photographers remain anonymous, the following are known to have taken certain of the pictures: Edward A. Standora, Joseph P. Schubauer, Gary B. Moran, Sylvia Greenwald, Robert R. Parmenter, Rebecca R. Sharitz, Justin D. Congdon, Judith L.

Greene, and Trip Lamb. Bud Harvey (DuPont Company) and Lt. Don Morrisey (Fort Gordon) also contributed photographs. My apologies to anyone who took a particular photograph and is not acknowledged here.

Their Blood Runs Cold

Adventures with Reptiles and Amphibians

Introduction

Two places in the United States have streams so hot that a person would die trying to swim them. One is Yellowstone National Park with its geysers, thermal springs, and the Firehole River. The other is more than two thousand miles away on the U.S. Department of Energy's Savannah River Plant (SRP) in South Carolina. The SRP has no natural heated waters, but the nation's plutonium production reactors create the only aquatic systems that can compete with Yellowstone's in terms of thermal alteration. Both places have waters hot enough to study the full spectrum of temperatures and conditions that can be encountered as a consequence of industrial releases of cooling water.

The SRP's nuclear reactors produce plutonium, in contrast to power reactors that generate electricity. Consequently, the cooling water, in its once-through passage, is not used to build up steam pressure. Instead, it is released directly into the aquatic environments at extremely high temperatures. Heated effluents are released into streams and reservoirs, creating thermal spectra that range as high as 160°F. (70°C.). One lake on the SRP has surface temperatures that can soft-boil an egg in two and a half minutes.

On July 1, 1967, I officially became one of the scientists at the University of Georgia's Savannah River Ecology Laboratory (SREL). I stayed on, beyond my two-year postdoctoral appointment, as a resident staff member because of the unsurpassed opportunities for many forms of ecological research related to the Southeast, particularly research with the cold-blooded terrestrial vertebrates, reptiles and amphibians—for I am a herpetologist first and an ecologist second. And to a herpetologist who is an ecologist the SRP is exceptional as the largest protected area of restricted-access land in the eastern United States.

Features of the SRP include a 2,800-acre reservoir on which the only boats are those of research scientists and one of the most apparent animals is the American alligator; a twenty-mile stretch of natural blackwater stream unpolluted from domestic, agricultural, or industrial sources, a fast vanishing habitat for untold numbers of water snakes; thirty square miles of one of the most beautiful cypress–tupelo gum swamps left in the South with some of the largest breeding populations of frogs and salamanders imaginable; and representatives of most of the natural habitats in the Atlantic Upper Coastal Plain. Terrestrial habitats include the natural sand-hill associations of longleaf pine and turkey oak with their pine snakes and racerunner lizards, hardwood forests that follow the corridors of the several salamander-laden natural streams, and more than a hundred Carolina bays, the natural wetland habitats of the Coastal Plain from Georgia to Virginia, in each of which literally thousands of semiaquatic turtles, snakes, frogs, and sala-manders spend all or part of their lives. Important man-made habitats also exist on the SRP: abandoned fields of varying ages up to twenty-five years, 100 million planted pine trees composing a variety of different aged stands, and a deserted town from which all human inhabitants left a quarter of a century ago. Each of these has its characteristic herpetofauna, too.

The SRP has features of which some people would not approve. For example, there is radioactive cesium in some parts of the cypress swamp. The thermal effluents have killed hundreds of large cypress and gum trees. And, the release of fly ash into one of the streams has caused the deaths of untold numbers of fish. But from the perspective of a research ecologist this situation is good because these events have been going on now for three decades, hand in hand with the natural environmental processes that have been occurring in contiguous habitats. In a paradoxical sense the SRP natural environments have been "saved" by the facility and the mode of operation. Thus, the SRP has become an outdoor laboratory permitting a comparison of natural systems with those influenced by human hands. For example, much of the cypress-gum swamp has been untouched by the thermal pollution but has been protected from the many other ravages of our highly exploit-ative society. Although unquestionable environmental disruption has occurred on the SRP, as an ecologist I see the SRP in a totally

Cypress stumps, remnants of trees killed a quarter of a century ago by heated water, still stand in the 150°F. effluent from a nuclear production reactor on the Savannah River Plant near Aiken, South Carolina. Although the waters swirling at their bases reach lethal temperatures, the stumps provide a viable substrate for invasion and colonization by other plant species, such as the seedling red maple shown in the foreground.

positive light as a research site. Ecology is a field within biology, which is the study of all facets of life; the goal of ecology, stated in simplest form, is to determine and understand the relationships that organisms have with their environments and with each other. More extensive, precise, or elaborate definitions can be formulated. Even more likely, the above definition can be variously interpreted. These variances reflect specialty interests and channeled perspectives.

This book is about ecology as a science and profession but as seen from the view of a herpetologist. Thus, the principal actors are reptiles and amphibians in today's world of rapidly changing environments. One fact that most of us surely would agree upon is that without a knowledge and understanding of ecology the people of any county, state, or country will be unable to make proper decisions about the many environments over which they now hold dominion. As a scientist, an ecologist, a herpetologist, I have spent most of my life keeping an account of the ecology of turtles, snakes, lizards, alligators, and salamanders, an activity through which I have been able to understand some things about ecology.

I have done ecological studies outside the realm of herpetology. They have been conducted so I could not only survive the pressures, constraints, and expectations of a scientific community that wants theories, principles, and concepts, but also satisfy government funding agencies that don't know what they want beyond the generality of something that's "relevant" to today's political outcries. But reptiles and amphibians have been the animals from which I have never strayed too far. Snakes are my favorite in the group. They hold the same fascination for me that they do for you. Most of us share an inexplicable fascination about snakes that makes some of us want to be involved with them and makes others want to avoid them at all cost.

Despite the pressures of colleagues and funding, I am no longer professionally afraid to admit that I really like snakes, have an affection for turtles, and feel proud when I catch an alligator. These are animals I like to work with and if principles and concepts are derived from my ecological work it will be because reptiles and amphibians hold the answers. As I have sought my answers through snakes and other reptiles, and amphibians, I have watched others get their answers through a diversity of organisms ranging from bats to canna lilies and cattails to crickets.

As ecologists we are working together to build the same pyramid with our own particular blocks, sometimes on different sides of the pyramid and from various angles. But each block is adding to the pyramid. So, as an ecologist prepares a block for the pyramid, he or she needs to keep an eye on the other blocks. That's what I've tried to do as I have helped add to the block of herpetology in the pyramid of ecology. In this book my purpose is simple and straightforward, that is, strictly for the entertainment of a reader who is interested in natural environments and in how a research ecologist who is a herpetologist studies them.

CHAPTER 1

Reptiles and Amphibians:

The Field of Herpetology

A reinforcement to me that ignorance about amphibians and reptiles in general and about snakes in particular prevails at all levels of education came at midnight in a small South Carolina hospital in July 1971. The scenario began four hours earlier with a phone call to my house. Dave, an undergraduate research participant, was calling from the Savannah River Ecology Laboratory to say that Rita, another student, had been bitten on the foot by a canebrake rattlesnake.

Full of the enthusiasm we instill in students for working with animals and meeting them on their own terms whenever possible, Dave, Rita, and a third student, Jim, had set out to do some road collecting earlier that evening. Patrolling the blacktop roads of the SRP for three hours, they had picked up two scarlet snakes and a corn snake. It wasn't raining so the only amphibians on the roads were toads who despise cold weather but seem to ignore the lack of moisture. The students had started early, at twilight, for that was the best time to find the normally crepuscular canebrake rattlesnake.

Everyone looks for the canebrake when they road collect in South Carolina. The canebrake is a prize. A trophy. You may come up with a justification for collecting specimens of one type or another, but every reptile-oriented herpetologist awaits the canebrake. It is a thrill seeker's species. And the three students found their thrill at 10:30 P.M.

Clipping along through the pine plantations, they had seen nothing for thirty minutes, save a fast-moving gray fox. Then they entered the valley of Upper Three Runs Creek. From the air the creek and its corridor of bottomland hardwoods appear to weave a sinuous path from the farmlands to the northeast across twenty miles of protected lands on the SRP. The hardwood corridor is a mile wide at some places and grades from annually flooded swamp forest habitat up into the dry-land oaks and hickories. Finally, at the top of the ridges, the smaller descendants of giant loblolly and longleaf pines now live.

The canebrake that got Rita could have crawled out from any of these places. As far as I can tell, canebrake rattlers are not as particular as most snakes about *where* they live. They are discriminating about *when*, however. A canebrake is seldom seen in the springtime in South Carolina before late April, although almost every other snake species will have already come and gone in number. Also, in the summer, canebrakes are nocturnal. They like to be out at night, but they do not care where they are, as long as mice, rats, and rabbits don't mind being there, too.

All three students saw the snake at the same time: a thin white line in the right lane, exactly perpendicular to the highway, with the front end elevated a few inches above the blacktop. Dave wheeled the gray government pickup to the left and braked as he went around. Knowing how things work when a bunch of herpetologists see a snake on the road, I'm sure there was a scramble for the flashlights and a snake stick. Everyone was probably being loud and imperative.

You have to hurry for most snakes, because they keep moving. And, at night, once they disappear into the grass on the shoulder of the road you most likely have lost them. But canebrakes are different. Canebrakes usually freeze when your headlights first shine on them, and they patiently lie and wait for you to get out of your truck. Not knowing this fact, however, Rita was in a big hurry.

As Dave backed up the truck, Rita opened the door, ready to jump. Running over a specimen when you're backing up is an embarrassment of the first order to a herpetologist. So, Dave stopped in the left lane before he had gone too far, he thought. Rita jumped out onto the highway.

Students enjoy going barefooted in the summer, and normally there is no problem as long as they don't mind the briers. But I now advise my students to be careful if they collect snakes and do not have on shoes—because that night Rita landed right in the middle of the rattlesnake's back. And who can blame the snake for what happened? The canebrake bit Rita on her big toe. I met the three students at the emergency entrance of the hospital, having already informed the night duty personnel that a snakebite victim was on the way.

The intern on duty, Dr. Plunt (the only fictitious name used in this book, for reasons that will become obvious), and I got our acquaintanceship off to a poor start when he reproachfully asked the students if they had brought the snake with them for identification. That was his mistake, founded on ignorance. My error was in pointing out his mistake to him. I told him that as long as it was not a coral snake, something anybody could identify, any poisonous snake in the South was a pit viper. The treatment for all of them is the same. They even use the same antivenin as a poison neutralizer.

Not surprisingly, he didn't like my intervention. After all, he was the doctor, as he said. I stated that I was too and that with a Ph.D. in zoology and a specialty in herpetology I had seen more snakebites than he had. It turned out to be true. This case was his first snakebite and my second.

As Rita stood by patiently, Dr. Plunt ended our exchange by storming through the door that led into the back of the emergency room. Over his shoulder he shouted some orders to the two nurses. One began to get out some surgical instruments as the other bathed Rita's foot.

The rest of us looked on to see how bad the swelling was. To be sure, the front part of her foot was red and plump. A tiny red pinhole could be seen in the center of her big toe. A fang mark. I looked carefully and concluded she had been hit by only one fang. In my estimation the probability of serious consequences immediately dropped to one-half. Also, the rattler had been a small one, further diminishing the chances of any real danger to Rita. In fact, if her disposition were any measure of the seriousness, one might think that nothing had happened. Rita was in a most agreeable mood and was bearing up exceptionally well for someone suffering from the pain of a poisonous snakebite. Even a minor bite like this one can be painful.

I began to relax and prepared myself to apologize to Dr. Plunt. I intended to explain to him that I had been tense because I was unaware that the bite was not a serious one. Yes, despite his officious nature, I truly was ready to apologize without pointing out his ignorance a second time—when he roared back into the emergency room brandishing a 20-ml syringe full of antivenin. All thought of apology vanished from my mind.

My level of anger and annoyance rose even higher when Dr. Plunt ignored me and did not answer my question about what he intended to do with the syringe and needle. Upon further inquiry, he finally answered that he was going to proceed with antivenin injections. When I began to admonish him for planning to administer antivenin without even examining the bite carefully, he lashed out at me by pointing out that he was a "real" doctor. I countered that I was the "real" doctor with my Ph.D. because the word *doctor* meant teacher and I had not seen him teach anything yet that was correct. I then went on to expound on the dangers of the horse serum–based antivenin and the potential for anaphylactic shock and other dread things about which I knew nothing.

When Dr. Plunt slammed the still-full syringe down on the counter and stormed into the back room again, I had the feeling of intellectual triumph. If he *really* knew what he was doing he would have proceeded with the injection. Obviously he was not confident about his stand. Within moments, though, an uneasiness came over me. Had I been overconfident? I only knew what I had read. Perhaps the bite was more serious than it seemed. A basic antibiotic and a painkiller should be all that is needed for many North American snakebites. Was this remedy really what Rita required? With an audience of three students and two nurses looking on, I certainly hoped so.

At that point I decided to meet the arrogance of ignorance face to face. Seeing Rita still in good spirits (over an hour had passed since the bite) and perceiving the uncertainty of the intern, I boldly declared that the bite was not even serious enough for Rita to stay in the hospital overnight. I went to tell Dr. Plunt.

As I pushed open the swinging door, a startled Dr. Plunt quickly stuffed a book into the drawer of the desk where he stood reading. He came toward me, declaring that he must begin cutting and suction. Again I was aghast, as this treatment was considered totally unnecessary under the conditions of minor swelling. He brushed past me, and I started to follow, to take my stand against overtreatment by the medical profession. But, when he went out the door, I did what you might have done. I went to the desk and opened the drawer. His medical source might be revealing.

And wasn't it! The *Boy Scouts of America Handbook!* The same edition that I had used two decades earlier while trying to get enough merit badges to keep my status in the neighborhood. The edition with the cover of a scout building a fire. Dr. Plunt was sneaking his information about snakebite treatment from an out-of-date scout handbook that only considered first aid in the field. I rushed back into the emergency room. It was not difficult to detect the apprehension that came over the faces of the other five as Dr. Plunt and I prepared for another showdown.

The handbook evidence was too embarrassing to mention with Dr. Plunt there, but I did declare what should be done. Antibiotics. A painkiller. A night's rest in the hospital under observation. He called my bluff by saying he would not prescribe anything while I was there. Furthermore, he declared that Rita was officially admitted into the hospital. The only way he would allow me to remain in her presence would be for me to sign a statement that I took full responsibility for her well-being and that she would then have to leave. In my opinion, this tactic was a low blow. But it didn't matter anymore. I took the bet and we all left, Rita hobbling between Dave and Jim.

Fortunately, in Rita's case I was holding the high hand. She took some aspirin that night and by the next afternoon the swelling had subsided. No secondary infection developed. Anything the doctor might have done certainly would have been overtreatment and potentially costly in more ways than one.

The whole scene scares me when I think back. Both of us, supposedly trained professionals, "doctors," were operating in a very dim light. My only saving grace was that I recognized his ignorance about the situation even though I was not sure about my own knowledge. Perhaps I was lucky, or Rita was, that my ignorance did not come into play in a manner that made a difference to her welfare.

Only after many years have I come to realize that certain knowledge must come from experience. Such is true of snakebite treatment, because each snake and each victim is a composite of numerous variables that affect the outcome. Because snakebite is a rare occurrence to the medical profession, most physicians in the

United States have never seen a snakebite victim. Hence they do not have experience on which to rely. Nor do we, the research ecologists and herpetologists, have experience that would be gained from extensive research on snakebite. Support for a rare medical problem such as snakebite cannot possibly command the research dollars that more visible problems such as cancer, heart disease, or diabetes do. Hence, in comparison, a minimal amount of medical research is done.

Snakebite is something that very few people, including professionals, know much about. But the entire realm of herpetology is in the same situation of wholesale ignorance not only in regard to most lay people but to the overwhelming majority of professional biologists, too. Of the five major classes of vertebrates, people know more about fishes, birds, and mammals than they do about reptiles and amphibians. This situation is evidenced in popular wildlife literature and in general discussions with people from all regions. Furthermore, the information that people provide about herpetofauna is misknowledge based on misinformation of various sorts or on such a limited supply of knowledge that misconception and superstition easily can be spawned. In my opinion, there are three primary reasons for the low emphasis placed on teaching and learning about reptiles and amphibians as compared to other vertebrates.

1. Few reptiles and amphibians have any commercial value as food or clothing, nor have they been essential to the welfare of a populace in a region; therefore, there has been little economic incentive to understand the life history or general biology of most species.
2. Because of the low numbers of species and the highly secretive nature of most forms of reptiles and amphibians, they are encountered far less frequently than the more numerous and obvious types of animals in this country.
3. The potential venomous nature of certain species of snakes and lizards and the man-eating tendencies of certain crocodilians have led to a psychological avoidance of these groups of animals. Uncharitable attitudes have extended to many non-dangerous species, including most lizards, most snakes, and

even a few completely harmless salamanders. The result is ignorance caused by an inclination not to be associated with these particular types of animals.

Each of these three reasons warrants discussion.

1. Commercial value—Only a few of the 450 species of reptiles and amphibians that occur in the United States have any significant commercial value. Although many species are edible, their small size or their success at being inconspicuous makes them unattractive from a commercial standpoint. A few species of reptiles and amphibians in this country have been exploited, however. In the nineteenth and early twentieth centuries, the diamondback terrapin, a coastal species of turtle ranging from Chesapeake Bay to the Gulf of Mexico, was commercially harvested and sold as a delicacy for soup or stew. At one time the Bureau of Commercial Fisheries even established a turtle-rearing program to see if this species could be raised successfully in captivity to provide for what appeared to be a rapidly flourishing market. As might be expected, the slow growth rate of individual turtles and long term (at least four years) for the females to reach maturity reduced the pursuit of this endeavor. Concomitantly the overexploitation in the coastal areas gradually reduced the turtle population to a point that a sufficient yield was no longer possible, and the use of diamondback terrapins for restaurant fare waned.

Likewise, certain of the marine turtles, such as the green turtle, occurred in southern coastal waters of the United States and once were heavily utilized as the base for turtle soup. Declining populations and the placement of most species onto legally endangered species lists put an end to this effort. Many turtles, of course, are eaten regionally, such as the chicken turtle in many parts of the South, the gopher tortoise in southern Georgia and Florida, and the various species of slider turtles in the eastern United States. The snapping turtle seems to be eaten throughout most of the United States. At best, however, turtle as a source of meat is a highly localized phenomenon.

Perhaps the most popular amphibian food source is frog legs. The legs of any frog would be satisfactory to eat, but in this country the only common species obtaining a size suitable for making a meal is the bullfrog. Attempts have been made to raise bullfrogs commercially in some parts of the South and in some instances thousands of pairs of legs per year have been sold for food.

Rattlesnake meat is still sold as a delicacy in parts of the South. Much of the supply comes as a result of the famed rattlesnake roundups in Georgia, Oklahoma, and other areas. Many species of snakes are edible, but only rattlesnakes attain a size large enough to obtain a sufficient supply of meat to make the effort of catching the animal and processing it worthwhile.

No lizards in the United States are considered a food source, although many species are edible. However, in Central and South America the large iguanas are a common food item of the natives of the region and are served in a variety of ways. The American alligator is a popular food with people who have eaten alligator tail. The meat is white, has the consistency of pork, and, if properly prepared, can be served as steaks. Legal limitations were imposed on this food item in 1973, by official placement of the alligator on the endangered species list throughout the country and by its remaining in endangered or threatened status in most regions.

Most herpetologists have had at least limited experience with eating their study organisms. Ernie Liner of New Orleans has published a book on the subject entitled *A Herpetological Cookbook: How to Cook Amphibians and Reptiles*. At SREL we have had our own experiences with some of the local fare at what we call the "Herp Dinners." The objective is to try to eat examples of all of the major groups of regional reptiles and amphibians with which we work. The animals used for food are taken primarily from specimens found recently killed on local highways or from specimens that were sacrificed in the laboratory as part of experiments.

The first Herp Dinner, in 1977, was an outstanding success. Besides the local graduate students, such as Bob Parmenter and Joe Schubauer who worked with turtles, and Pat Murphy who studied alligators, we had visiting herpetologists from Michigan (Don Tinkle and Justin Congdon), Texas (Gary Ferguson), and Chicago (Ken Derickson). The final spread was magnificent and included sautéed alligator tail (legally obtained and frozen in 1971 after a large male was killed by a logging truck); legs of bullfrogs, leopard frogs, and green frogs; snapping turtle salad (excellent on crackers); slider turtle stew; crispy fried mole salamanders; baked canebrake rattlesnake (a 4½-foot specimen coiled around tomatoes and green peppers); and deep-fried strips of cottonmouth moccasin. Although all of the representatives were unusual compared to a typical American meal, two of the items stood out in uniqueness and were declared to be the best and worst of the evening.

The "best" was a consequence of our having collected thirty-six male banded water snakes at a place called Flamingo Bay the night before. Even with eight of us walking around in the water, a total of forty-seven snakes (the thirty-six males plus nine females and two cottonmouth moccasins) was a lot to catch in one night. And fortunately they filled our need for a sample of water snakes to dissect to determine reproductive and lipid cycles in the species. During the Herp Dinner the following night we served part of the sample as hors d'oeuvres that were as well received as Oysters Bienville or Crab Louis. Everyone loved them and complained bitterly when the seventy-two "swamp oysters" as we called them were all gone. Only later did Bob Parmenter and I reveal that we had served perhaps the largest appetizer tray of water snake testes ever eaten in the United States. Let me repeat, though, they were excellent!

The "worst" item of the night had no close contestant. Gary Ferguson disappeared from the room "ill" after the first bite, and none of us was able to swallow any. The food was fried blue-tailed skink, one of the three species of local lizards with a brilliant blue tail. Although none of us has published on the subject in the scientific literature, we did conclude that to less naive predators than ourselves an attractive blue tail probably serves as a warning that a skink does not taste good.

We have continued the Herp Dinners at SREL, experiencing such new entrées as Laurie Vitt's soft-shell turtle casserole and Trip Lamb's snapper gumbo. Despite the appeal of herps as unusual delicacies, their exploitation for such purpose on a grand scale is never likely to be profitable.

Besides their use as food, reptiles and amphibians also have been commercially exploited for other purposes. Certain salamanders, for example, are sold as fish bait in some areas. The most apparent impact on a North American reptile species was the exploitation of the American alligator for hides to make shoes, belts, and purses, resulting in the elimination of the species in many parts of its range during the mid-1900s. In addition many species of reptiles and amphibians have been, and still are, sold as pets, although this practice is based mostly on incidental captures of various species. One market that is no longer in effect is the sale of baby turtles, primarily painted turtles and certain species of slider and map turtles. The demise of this market was partially a consequence of their being implicated as carriers of *Salmonella*, a form of bacteria that causes a severe intestinal ailment. Nonetheless, despite these few examples of commercial uses of herpetofauna, the impact on the commercial market has been trivial compared to that of mammals, birds, and fishes, although the impact on the animals themselves has in many instances been severe.

2. Secretive nature—In a scientific sense, reptiles and amphibians are no more closely related than reptiles and birds, yet their study is combined into a single field, herpetology. The word comes from the Greek word *herpeton*, meaning "creeping thing," and sums up one of the qualities that link the Class Reptilia and Class Amphibia. Most species indeed can be ascribed as creepers, which combined with another trait, smallness, leads to a general characteristic of being clandestine. This overall feature of secretiveness is a major reason why reptiles and amphibians are artificially included together in a single field, whereas fishes, birds, and mammals are studied separately. That is, reptiles and amphibians are superficially similar in their selection of habitats and are likely to be found in the same kinds of places. In many areas, when you turn over a log in the woods you are as likely to find a reptile as an amphibian. Because they are found together, they are studied together.

The actual numbers of species of any major group of animals can never be known for sure but accurate estimates have been made for the vertebrates. Amphibians are at one end of the species scale, with only about 3,000 representatives worldwide, whereas fishes with over 17,000 species are at the other. The world contains about twice as many kinds of reptiles (6,000 species) as amphibians, more than the mammals (about 3,500 species) but fewer than the birds (about 8,600 species).

Relative to the other vertebrates, reptiles and particularly amphibians are inconspicuous far beyond what might be expected on the basis of the numbers of species or individuals that are present in an area. Even though the mountains of Tennessee and North Carolina have the greatest concentrations of salamanders in the world, many southerners have never even seen a salamander. The explanation is simple. Most salamanders are small and inconspicuous to begin with and the habit of most is to live underground or under leaf litter or other forest debris for the majority of their lives. When they do venture forth, it is usually on rainy nights, a time when nonherpetologists are least likely to be out.

The fact that few people like to get outside their living rooms on a rainy night, particularly when it involves going into a swamp or woody area, is one reason that people are not more aware of how many frogs occupy most parts of the country. In short, the behavioral habits of most humans do not overlap at all with the behavioral activities of most frogs. Who is likely to hear a breeding chorus of two hundred spring peepers on a cold rainy night in February along the Atlantic seaboard or the ceaseless quacking of a thousand green tree frogs during a summer thunderstorm on a barrier island? When daylight comes and the humans emerge, the frogs are all gone, buried deep beneath the vegetation, mud, or other hiding places until the right nighttime conditions occur for them to emerge again. Most frogs are this way, being active mostly at night and making a racket that calls attention to themselves primarily when it is raining. Otherwise they are quiet and inconspicuous during the times when humans are active.

Turtles are perhaps the most conspicuous of the reptiles or amphibians because of the propensity of a few species to bask in the sun where people can see them. Most turtles are very shy and quick to retreat into the water off a log if they are disturbed. But some species congregate in large numbers in certain areas if they go unmolested. Also, almost everyone has seen a box turtle in those parts of the United States where they occur, wandering through the woods or alongside roads or sometimes making the fatal mistake of trying to cross one. So turtles really do not qualify for the same level of inconspicuousness that most of the other reptiles and amphibians do.

Snakes have their own style of secretiveness, much of which comes from staying out of view throughout most of their lives. In some of the snake-dense areas of the country, such as the Southeast, people may spend their whole lives living in an area where

Dr. Donald W. Tinkle, who died of cancer in 1979, was one of the most outstanding field herpetologists in the world. His classic studies on the evolutionary ecology of reptiles are known by all professional herpetologists and students. He inspired numerous students at all levels to ask questions that were best answered by working directly with animals in their natural habitats.

thirty to forty kinds of snakes occur and yet may never see more than half a dozen different kinds in their life. Part of the snakes' secretiveness comes from actually hiding underground or concealing themselves in various ways. But many snakes go unseen because most people are inexperienced in spotting them, even when they are close at hand, because of effective patterns of color and camouflage. Lizards likewise are frequently in view to people but go unseen because of effective camouflage.

So, despite the obviousness of a few reptiles, such as basking turtles and large snakes, most reptiles and amphibians cannot compare with the ever-present birds and fishes for conspicuousness. Mammals indeed are more secretive in nature than fishes or birds but, if one considers the numbers of squirrels, rabbits, mice, and occasional opossums and deer that we see, the herpetofauna are definitely in last place in terms of being seen by people.

3. Psychological avoidance—Most people tend to avoid anything that is threatening, distasteful, or unpleasant in some way. Avoidance of a subject maintains ignorance about it and is perhaps one reason why reptiles and amphibians are so poorly understood. It is no myth that certain snakes and at least two species of crocodiles have been responsible for numerous human deaths. This fact scares people: to think that a lower life form can callously kill or even eat a human. Consequently, the most prudent approach has been considered to be one of keeping a safe distance from such creatures that show themselves to be cold-blooded in more ways than one. Such an attitude, based on fear, is unlikely to promote knowledge of the animals in question.

Reptiles intentionally cause human deaths in three different ways. The most common and well-known means whereby certain snakes and two southwestern lizards can kill people is by means of injection of venom. All of the warm continents have poisonous snakes, capable of giving a lethal bite. This fact probably has resulted in a mindset in many cultures that all snakes can be dangerous—for rather than attempt to learn which ones are poisonous and which ones are not, it usually has been easier to avoid all snakes and to teach others to do the same. This notion has no doubt been the safest approach for individual humans and for the culture but not for the harmless species of snakes.

Other examples of reptiles that have killed people are the Nile crocodile of Africa and the saltwater crocodile of the Australian-Malaysian region of the world. Both of these species unquestionably and unremorsefully will devour a human being if the circumstances are suitable. The mentality of a saltwater crocodile, which does, incidentally, come far inland into fresh water, appears to be no different from that of a great white shark when it feeds. Therefore, a human who is small enough for the crocodile to handle is fair game. Unfortunately, a saltwater crocodile may reach a length of more than twenty feet and can have a jaw length of more than two feet. Needless to say, no human is a match to such an animal. These Old World crocodiles have given a lot of bad press to their New World relatives, none of which is particularly dangerous unless provoked or cornered. Americans have been trying for decades to indict the American alligator as a killer. But American alligators are like house pets compared to the Old World man-eaters.

The final example of intentional killing by a reptile is the case of the large constrictors. A few cases are on record of South American anacondas and some of the Old World pythons (snakes reaching lengths of more than twenty-five feet) having attacked, killed by constriction, and then eaten humans, usually children. No poisonous snake ever has been known to eat a person. Despite the few tragic instances of large constrictors' eating or attempting to eat humans, among the reptiles only the two species of Old World crocodiles can be accused of making humans a regular part of their diet through the ages.

Amphibians, of course, do not kill people. Hellbenders, the large ugly salamanders living in mountain streams of the eastern United States, sometimes are thought to be poisonous but are harmless. The secretions from the enlarged poison glands located behind the head of some toads are deadly poisonous in large quantity and, indeed, there are records of dogs dying after biting a toad. However, these occurrences are unintentional on the part of the toad so do not qualify in the category of what snakes or man-eating crocodiles are capable of.

Limited commercial value, an inherent inconspicuousness, and fear-provoking capabilities of some species all contribute to why reptiles and amphibians are poorly known and why herpetology is undertaught. Yet, ironically, the members of the groups, particularly some of the reptiles, hold a fascination for people that is unparalleled by most other members of the animal or plant kingdoms. Herpetology captivates us, perhaps, because for most people, even highly educated ones, any entry into the field is an adventure into the unknown.

CHAPTER 2

The Snakes:

Once Upon a Bushmaster

The first snake I can remember was a green snake that lay outstretched on the largest limb of a redbud tree in Alabama. We smashed it many times. To death. Making sure. Taking no chances.

I don't really think I cried that night, but I do remember that I didn't feel right afterward. I distinctly remember that at five years old I did not feel good about killing my first snake.

Fifteen years later as R. E. Smith and I walked through a Costa Rican jungle in search of frogs, the serpents had a chance to even the score (or in the words of God, to "bruise my heel"). We were kicking the grass in a clearing to make the frogs jump. When we saw one we pounced fast and stuffed our quarry into a cloth collecting bag. I was still killing animals, but for science, and for someone else. At the time I did not really appreciate why. That would come later.

One might have guessed that when we left The University of Alabama the following year, R. E. would be the one to go to Harvard for graduate school. Why else was *I* the one in low-cut sneakers leading the way through the jungle while he followed behind wearing shin-high combat boots? Was he giving me every opportunity to catch the most animals?

The toes in my left foot have held a place of honor for the rest of my body ever since that day—for I did not see the coiled, nine-foot bushmaster until my right heel touched the top of its head. Any toes that could take a 160-pound student and send him backward with the speed of light are indeed special.

Much of my body got into the act. My mouth spoke, very loud. My pancreas felt a jolt from my adrenal gland output. My lungs and heart did what they were supposed to do, and the back of my right hand accidentally whapped R. E. squarely in the nose, causing his horn-rims to go flying. Rolling like a paratrooper and abandoning all teachings that I gave to others that pit vipers will not chase you and that all snakes are slow (even the fastest coachwhips and black racers have been recorded to travel less than five miles an hour), I spun through the grass. Two small frogs cleared out of my path and I gave fleeting thought that I might have discovered a new collecting technique. I rolled on past Raoul, our ever-silent Costa Rican guide. I was not sure whether he stood in awe of me or the snake. But once behind him I knelt to evaluate the situation.

Raoul stood entranced, holding his rifle at his side, as always. A safe distance of twenty feet separated me and Raoul from the bushmaster. But I felt as though my heart had stopped, and my blood ran cold, if those things really happen, when I saw R. E.

Apparently inattentive to my shouts, or at least to their meaning, he had set about to find his glasses. The fact that R. E. would grope through the grass on all fours directly toward a nine-foot bushmaster attests to his need to have them on. The snake must have been as amazed at our antics as Raoul was, for it lay in silent coil as R. E. fished around with his hands, not four feet away.

Not relishing the idea of being partial cause to the envenomation and sure death of a potential Harvard graduate student, I rushed back to where he was. Raoul and the snake both seemed captivated by the show. Neither moved as I yanked R. E. backward by the shoulders and then dragged him several feet through the grass. I was truly sorry about having stepped on R. E.'s glasses during this part of the event, but to me the most critical item on the ground was a bushmaster as fat as a football.

Bushmasters are elegant snakes, and even in my early ignorance I knew something of them. As the largest poisonous snakes in the Western Hemisphere and the largest pit vipers in the world, they have an awesome reputation. Approaching twelve feet in length, some may have fangs more than an inch long. The color varies, but the basic pattern is one of an overall light brown, yellowish, or pinkish with a row of rhomboids that look like black felt down the back. Of the dozens of New World pit vipers the bushmaster is the only species that lays eggs. Its generic name, *Lachesis*, is appropriate because Lachesis was the Fate who measured the thread of life. *Lachesis* has measured many threads in tropical America.

Now, with R. E. rescued and both of us unharmed, my own thread seemed longer. I began to plan my counterattack. With the possibility of death put momentarily on a backburner, one thought stood foremost in my mind. We had to catch that snake!

This time on my trip back to the snake I tried to wrest the rifle from Raoul. You would have thought that taking a gun from a statue would be easy. But when I pulled, both Raoul and the rifle came forward. He didn't pull back, but he wouldn't let go either. He never so much as looked at me, although I shouted loud commands that he must do so instantly. Raoul just stared at the bushmaster, entranced beyond consciousness.

Finally I won the rifle by flinging Raoul to one side, directly into R. E., who was edging forward with the caution of a myopic man on the edge of a cliff. They both went down into the grass with R. E. giving loud inquiry as to the status of his glasses.

I rushed forward, intending to shoot the monster between the eyes. But things changed fast that day. The coiled snake was gone! A fleeting arrow of fear shot through me as I realized I could be standing on top of, or certainly within striking range of, a pair of long fangs backed by some hefty poison glands. Then I saw it again, gliding across the last of the grass carpet into a cane patch that bordered the jungle. The camouflage was magnificent. While this deadly creature need have little concern about predators, it makes its living by not being seen by prey.

As I moved into the cane thicket, the reeds in front of me swayed in a sinuous path for several feet. I was impressed that a snake could visibly affect shoulder-high bamboo in so noticeable a fashion. The bushmaster was not slowing down, and I had to be careful lest it stopped and I overran the body and caught up with its head. Sometimes even a nonpoisonous snake, like a racer or coachwhip, when pursued too closely will stop and turn on its attacker, ready to bite. So I paced myself, ready to make my move with the rifle when the animal reached a small clearing between the bamboo and the jungle. Circling off to the side, I planned to meet it head on when it emerged from the cane.

Seconds later, I got my chance. Out came a head as big as a combat boot. I aimed for the brain, right between the eyes with their sinister-looking vertical pupils. One shot will always do it, even with a big snake, if your aim is good. And a single bullet will leave only a small hole, doing only slight visible damage to the skull. Only then did I discover that Raoul carried no bullets in his rifle. I don't know how high I jumped when I realized my would-be quarry was going right between my legs, but when I landed, all nine feet of deadly bushmaster had passed me by. I threw the rifle into the cane patch and pulled out my machete. Machetes are essential in the bush of that region so we each carried one. Even five-year-old children dragged their sheathed machetes in the sand beside them. I would get one last chance.

As I poised to strike, I considered the possibilities. The snake was disappearing fast into the thicket where I could no longer follow without great effort and danger. About four and a half feet of snake was still in the clearing. I knew that one solid whack with that blade would leave the harmless half of a bushmaster thrashing in the clearing and the deadly end in the jungle facing a sure death within minutes. I could find the jungle half in short order, once I knew it was dead.

My arm tensed for the swing, and I took a fleeting look at my two companions. Raoul was standing mouth open, eyes staring at some point in space in the vicinity of me and *Lachesis*. R. E. was crouched, searching the grass for his lost and, unknown to him, broken glasses. He must have discovered them that very instant, because he clamped his hands atop his head and fell to the earth with a scream to investigate their shattered remains. The rifle lay in the reed patch behind me and nine-tenths of the adrenalin in my body was a consequence of fear rather than bravery. I was about to kill this snake in a less than honorable manner. No. I could not do it. *Lachesis* had won this one. I watched the last of the beautiful tail disappear into the jungle darkness. It looked purple and buff in the fading light.

I have been in the land of the ignorant many times and know that in many categories I am still there. But in herpetology a change has occurred. I've watched the light come in, ever so gradually, I admit; in looking back I see my own early ignorance of snakes and many poor decisions because of it. Today I am of course glad that Raoul had no bullets, for all I would have now is the head of a magnificent bushmaster, with a small hole in it, and maybe its skin. Both would be stored away in a museum cabinet for few eyes to see. Do not misunderstand. The collection of museum specimens for study is a worthy scientific endeavor by those who know what they are doing. The preservation of specimens in a selective, judicious manner is essential and must be carried on. But *Lachesis*'s head (we did not have enough formaldehyde to pickle the body of a large snake) would have been no more than a trophy. I nearly had that trophy, then lost it through no decision of my own when I pulled the trigger. But I feel good that the second time, brandishing my machete, I chose to concede on my own.

Too many times I had brought home the environmental trophies, thoughtlessly, in ignorance or selfishness in one form or another. Too many times the gun had been loaded. Or, too many times I had not taken advantage of the second chance. Giant pit vipers are becoming rare and their wanton destruction along with that of bowhead whales or whooping cranes or saguaro cacti will rob us of a heritage and guarantee us nothing for the future.

Bushmasters in particular have a rare standing in our evolutionary heritage because of their unique biological features and uncertain phylogenetic origin. The small temporary gain to the ego of one human specimen scarcely could have made up for the loss suffered ecologically through the killing of this single specimen of *Lachesis*. The true gain of the day was the stirrings of a shift in environmental attitude from total ecological ignorance to at least an awareness that we must share the world with other creatures. The greatest loss of the day was R. E.'s glasses.

The bushmaster escaped that day in Costa Rica and not entirely because of my good will or intentions. But it fared better than thousands of other snakes do each year, poisonous or not. Most people in the United States have rather harsh mindsets about what the most satisfactory condition of a "good" snake is. Intentional, as well as unintentional, killing of snakes is proceeding at an alarming rate throughout the country. Highway deaths are one way human activity impacts on this poorly understood group of animals. But each new dam construction, timber removal operation, drained swamp, and housing or resort development leads to the reduction in the numbers of some of the more than 110 species of snakes in the United States. Poisonous species attract a lot of attention because of the potential harm they can do us. But have you considered what we humans do to harm the snakes, including the

Once Upon a Bushmaster • 23

almost four dozen harmless varieties in the East? Unfortunately, human beings through their influence on the environment are the greatest threat to all snakes, harmless or not. And snakes are only the example that I have chosen to indicate our national attitude toward many of the subtle but important components of natural environments.

We probably have our greatest effect on snakes, as well as on all other animals and plants, by altering their habitats. Although a species' geographic range includes a particular area, unless the habitat and other environmental conditions are right the animal probably will not be there. Habitat change is inevitable. But, what might occur in a million years under natural conditions can be brought about in a week by an enthusiastic bulldozer operator or logging crew. Within a few years, a forest can change from hardwood to pure pine; a river and its floodplain can become a reservoir. Although species adapt to new environments over evolutionary time, rapid destruction of their habitats unquestionably reduces the species diversity by eliminating those forms that cannot adjust to the sudden confrontation of a new environment.

Habitat destruction can be observed by the gradual loss of the eastern indigo snake from major portions of its range. Once reported from South Carolina, this largest of North American snakes has not been found there in almost forty years and now is recognized as an endangered species in Florida, Alabama, and Georgia. Indigo snakes are found in extensive tracts of undeveloped sand ridge habitat. Unfortunately, few large undisturbed areas remain, and if these magnificent snakes are still with us in South Carolina the survivors will be in what's left of this habitat in the southern reaches of the state.

Most would agree that some snake species seem to be disappearing rapidly throughout the United States because of human activities. A reduction in numbers is certain for many species that have specialized requirements of diet or habitat. Documentation of the effects of habitat alteration on snakes is difficult because few careful studies have been carried out to determine abundance and diversity of species in an area. The impressions and predictions of experts in the field of herpetology can provide some insight into the extent of this problem, but the ecology of almost every species of snake in the world is so poorly known that herpetologists can only speculate about what the fate of each has been in the environmental exhaust of human progress.

A few species in the Southeast unquestionably have suffered:

Yellow rat snake. In the Carolinas this subspecies of the black rat snake (or chicken snake) is restricted to the barrier islands and adjoining coastal mainland. The rapid development of the coastal region has already had and will have a major impact on this species as a consequence of habitat destruction.

Pine snake. This impressive constrictor inhabiting the once-vast natural pine and scrub oak regions of the East preys primarily on rats, mice, and (sometimes) birds. Today its preferred habitats, already much diminished by early lumbering and farming endeavors, continue to fall prey to other enterprises. The sandy habitats are often suitable for the development of pine plantations or suburban residential areas. Neither seems to serve as a suitable habitat for pine snakes.

Queen snake. A specialized diet of stream crayfish probably makes this species' ecology too fragile to cope with certain dredging or damming projects. A safe bet is that the construction of each dam in the range of queen snakes greatly reduces their preferred habitat (small streams) and eliminates many populations of the species.

Eastern diamondback rattlesnake. The march of civilization along the East Coast has eliminated many of the favored palmetto habitats of this species. But, intentional removal of specimens, especially large adults, by collectors may be reducing their numbers even more. Several southern states attract snake collectors from afar, and the diamondback is one of the most sought-after prizes. Perhaps the most ruthless form of destruction of this fierce but noble snake is the gassing of specimens where they hibernate in the burrows of gopher tortoises. The "rattlesnake roundups" of southern Georgia and Oklahoma are not very pretty sights, particularly if you care anything about the several kinds of animals that succumb to the onslaught.

Scarlet kingsnake. Herpetologists know so little about some species of snakes that no data-based judgment can be made about how human activities affect them. One of these species deserves special mention because, in the opinion of many herpetologists, it is the most beautiful snake in the eastern United States and is also one of the most infrequently collected. However, many "rare" species occur abundantly in selected areas under certain circumstances and indeed the scarlet kingsnake has such a place near Ocotee, South Carolina. Hundreds of snake collectors once came to Ocotee every spring. As many as two hundred, possibly more, "scarlet kings" are known to have been removed in a single week. Most were sold to pet dealers or to individuals with snake collections at home for as much as $100 each. Fortunately, public access to that unusual collecting site no longer is allowed.

The examples mentioned above demonstrate the ways in which some snakes are slowly being driven from their habitats. The gradual loss of any component of an ecosystem should serve as a warning. Perhaps the snakes are only indicators of deeper-lying trouble.

In the complex environmental network of a region, snakes play the role of predator. All snakes throughout the world are strict carnivores, but some species are much more selective than others. Snakes often represent the last line of control for certain prey species, particularly mice and rats, whose numbers might otherwise increase in an area. To their credit, many farmers are well aware that a rat snake, corn snake, or kingsnake in the vicinity of the corncrib dramatically cuts down the number of rodent pests. Laboratory studies indicate that an adult of any of these species easily can consume ten mice or rats per week. Because there are at least twenty-five weeks a year when snakes are active in most parts of the United States, a single snake can reduce significantly the number of such pests in an area. Without question, each rodent-eating snake in the United States dispenses with dozens of rats and mice during a single year. Some snake species, however, as dietary specialists, are potentially susceptible to population reduction in response to any natural or man-caused reduction in their primary prey. For example, rainbow snakes primarily eat eels and salamanders, and queen snakes predominantly eat crayfish.

But having feeding habits that are different from those of most other animals is one reason for the image that snakes have. The following scene exemplifies the approach of some species.

The fanlike canopy of the palmetto fronds created a shadowy gloom in the fading light of early evening. Even the keenest-eyed observer might not have seen the coiled form that blended into the brown of the dead vegetation at the plant's base. The yellowish stripes on the brown face could be mistaken for the last streaks of sunlight that had crept into the pine and palmetto forest of central Florida. The yellow-rimmed diamonds likewise gave the appearance of a sun-and-shade mixture.

The occasional flick of a forked tongue was the only clue that life dwelled beneath the green of the palmetto. The pair of unblinking eyes stared forward, alert but patient, waiting for the next meal.

The large rat that scurried through the underbrush searching for seeds or insects was old enough to know better. Having spent its lifetime trying to avoid becoming a meal, it should have been more cautious when it approached the palmetto plant with an obvious hiding place for a snake. Perhaps the previous evening's close encounter with an early-rising barred owl had made the rat more aware of predators in the air rather than those on the ground.

The flash of fangs emerging from the shadows brought instant but short-lived terror to the rat, for the lightning strike had been dead on its mark. The rat quivered in its tracks and within a minute moved no more. The rattlesnake's forked tongue questioned the safety of the situation by seeking chemical information before it left the palmetto's base and consumed the prey.

Although this lifestyle may seem violent, perhaps even cruel to some, a snake is an efficient and prudent predator. Except in instances of defensive behavior, snakes kill animals only for food. Snakes never overeat in natural situations and their methods of killing are usually quick and effective. But unlike birds with their beaks and claws, snakes are limited in the weapons they have to make a living in the dynamic world of nature.

Imagine if you had to get your food and protect yourself with no arms or legs. That's the dilemma of all snakes, without any friends to help. Therefore many of the remarkable features about snakes involve food-getting and protection. To us their most obvious adaptation is the poison apparatus. Its primary function as a

The three common pit vipers of the eastern United States are the copperhead, cottonmouth moccasin, and canebrake (or timber) rattlesnake. Other pit vipers east of the Mississippi are the eastern diamondback rattlesnake of the coastal South, the pygmy rattlesnake, and the massasauga of the Midwest. The coral snake, a member of the cobra family, is the only other poisonous snake species in the East. The western United States has more than a dozen poisonous species, most of which are rattlesnakes.

Copperhead. The copperhead, a handsome "highland" relative of the cottonmouth, has a brown and copper banding pattern that resembles dead leaves of autumn. Copperheads are the least dangerous of the poisonous snakes in the eastern United States, although they are responsible for numerous bites in the more mountainous and rocky areas. They may be found in almost any habitat. The corn snake and some water snakes have similar red or coppery banding patterns and often are mistaken for the poisonous species.

Eastern diamondback rattlesnake. The king of the poisonous snakes east of the Mississippi River is the eastern diamondback rattlesnake. Adults of this species are the most dangerous snakes in the South. Diamondbacks are predominantly coastal and do not come far inland. A big one may reach a length of eight feet and be as thick as a man's leg. With fangs long enough to penetrate an inch beneath the skin, diamondbacks can deliver venom in twice the quantity of most other species in the United States. Coastal development has destroyed much of the diamondbacks' habitat and the enormous ones are seldom encountered anymore.

Canebrake rattlesnake. The rattlesnake of most widespread occurrence in the East is the canebrake or timber rattler, a large species that can be more than five feet long. The southern variety, known as the canebrake, has an orange stripe down the back. Normally canebrakes have a grayish body with black chevrons and a velvety black tail tipped with rattles. Canebrakes are usually docile animals when not molested, but a big one is dangerous, so extreme caution should be taken when one is encountered. The best action to take with any poisonous snake is total avoidance.

Cottonmouth. The cottonmouth moccasin is the most abundant poisonous snake in aquatic habitats of the Southeast. Description is difficult because of extensive variation in color pattern from orange or copper banding as a baby, to olive, brown, or dull black as an adult. An additional complication in recognizing cottonmouths in the wild is that several species of large, equally abundant and nondescript water snakes (all mean in disposition, but harmless) occupy the same wet area environments as do cottonmouths. But, rather than try to identify every specimen in wet habitats, the best approach is to leave all of them alone.

Coral snake. The only poisonous snake of the Southeast that is not a pit viper is the famous coral snake with its red, yellow, and black–ringed body. Although beautiful, the eastern coral snake has venom equivalent in potency to that of a cobra. Because of their small size and inefficient venom injection systems, few deaths by coral snakes have been confirmed in the United States.

feeding mechanism often is overshadowed by the secondary use as a defensive device. Eighteen species of snakes in the United States are poisonous to humans. Of these, fourteen are rattlesnakes, of which ten are restricted to the Southwest. Although humans seem to take it personally that a few snakes are poisonous, the venom mechanism serves functions far beyond that of intimidating even the boldest Texas rancher. Many animals make their living by eating anything that doesn't eat them first, and the poison threat has saved many a rattler, cottonmouth, or copperhead from becoming a meal to raccoons, foxes, or even skunks. Poison is merely a defense, and we are particularly aware of it because it is effective against us as well as other animals. Every snake species has some form of defense against the rest of the world, but only a small proportion (16 percent in the United States) are effectively venomous to humans. So, what do the others do?

Perhaps the most common defensive strategy among snakes, particularly small ones, is secretiveness. In fact, one reason for the common misconception that most snakes are poisonous is that few people are aware of the number of snake species that are literally underfoot and never seen. A group of little brown snakes, known to herpetologists as crowned snakes because of their black heads, occur throughout the southern United States. The southeastern crowned snake probably occurs abundantly in every woodland habitat in the Southeast. Yet ask 1,000 southerners if they have ever seen one. Chances are that 990 have not. The reason is that crowned snakes, along with worm snakes, ringneck snakes, and numerous other species of "ground snakes," spend their lives beneath the ground or under surface litter. The average human is likely to encounter them only during a gardening venture or yard raking. Because of their small size and obscure appearance (many species look like a piece of brown spaghetti), even those uncovered may not be seen.

Subterranean lifestyles understandably result in certain snakes' being effectively invisible, but even those that spend much of their life above ground have their ways of going unseen. Camouflage has been perfected by many animals that make good meals, including snakes. A moving green vine may be your only clue that a green snake is on an ivy-covered wall or a honeysuckle-shrouded hedgerow. Or, consider the blending quality of the dull brown and gray patterns of the harmless water snakes that live in dimly lit swamps or along stream margins. Even the poisonous forms take advantage of camouflage. The autumn-leaf pattern and color of the woodland copperhead or the sand color of the desert-dwelling sidewinder rattlesnake might at first make one wonder why they need be poisonous.

But protection is not the only reason for a limbless creature to be poisonous. Snakes must eat, and being able to go unnoticed and then subdue prey with one bite is a worthwhile trait for an organism that eats only living animals. In fact, when it comes to food getting, in contrast to protection, many snakes that are harmless to humans are deadly to such creatures as earthworms or lizards. The inoffensive crowned snakes, although seemingly incapable and certainly uninterested in biting a human finger, have tiny fangs and poison sacs in the rear of their mouths that are used in paralyzing small invertebrate prey. Certain snakes of the Southwest, such as the California lyre snake, similarly possess enlarged rear teeth and poisonous saliva capable of overcoming their main food source, lizards or small mammals. Numerous such semipoisonous snakes occur throughout the world, particularly in tropical areas. In Australia, over half of the more than one hundred species of snakes belong to the cobra family, but many are not in any way dangerous to even a child because their venom mechanism and potency are designed for feeding and not for defense.

The other well-known approach used by snakes to obtain and hold food is constriction. Pythons and anacondas, the giant snakes of the Old and New World tropics, respectively, are the best-known actors along with their smaller (usually less than fifteen feet long) relative, the boa constrictor of Central America. Their act is simple and little different from that of the rat snakes, kingsnakes, and bull snakes of the United States. Constrictors grab their prey while still alive and with the speed of a rattlesnake's strike they throw as many coils of their body as possible around the animal. Death comes from suffocation. Besides the traditional style of encircling the victim with a series of powerful coils, a variety of other pressure tactics are used by snakes. A coachwhip does not constrict its prey but will press a mouse or rat against the ground with its body, sometimes holding three or four in place at the same time. Incidentally, one fact that seems to escape adventure story

The head of a rattlesnake demonstrates how venom is administered to a victim by a pit viper. Poison glands are located near the back of the head. The impact of biting and pressure from compressor muscles force poison from the sacs through venom ducts into the hollow fangs. An opening in the tip of the fangs allows the system to operate in the same manner as a hypodermic syringe. The movable fangs lie parallel to the roof of the mouth when the mouth is closed. The heat-sensitive "pit" of a pit viper is located between and slightly below the eye and nostril. Rattlesnakes are the most formidable poisonous snakes in the parts of the United States where they occur.

illustrators for pulp magazines is that no poisonous snake in the world is also a constrictor that wraps around its victim.

Besides constriction and poison, certain snakes have special techniques for obtaining their prey. The Central American snail-eating snakes have elongated lower jaws to reach into the shell, making escargot dining look easy. The egg-eating snakes of Africa have numerous enlarged bony spines projecting internally into the throat from the neck vertebrae. The spines intercept a swallowed egg, break it, and allow the snake to consume the contents of an egg much larger than the snake's own diameter and to disgorge the shell fragments. In the United States, the eastern hognose snake specializes in dining on common terrestrial toads, species that respond to predation by puffing their bodies up like a big bag of air. Most snakes, even with their elastic mouths and stretchable bodies, often are unable to consume what at first appears to be an easy meal. But the hognose circumvents the whole issue with a pair of elongated teeth that are pressed into the side of the toad and simply let the air out of the balloon.

But of all the unusual forms of protection and food getting by snakes, none surpasses venom in attracting attention. Poison injection is done most dramatically by the vipers and pit vipers, which have large, curved fangs that fold back into sheaths when the mouth is closed. The fangs on a large bushmaster of South America may approach two inches in length and have the impact of a pair of ice picks when they enter the skin. The fangs of members of the cobra family, including the coral snakes, kraits, and mambas, are small and straight, although drop for drop the venom may be far more potent than that of most vipers and pit vipers. The sea snakes, normally inoffensive coastal or, in some instances, ocean-going creatures, also are equipped with relatively small fangs but have some of the most toxic venom of any creature. According to one study conducted for the U.S. Navy, the venom of a sea snake was found to be 1,000 times more deadly than that of the copper-head.

One unique approach to venom delivery is that of the spitting cobras of Africa, which squeeze the poison through openings in the front of their fangs with such force that the liquid may go a distance of several feet. An encounter with a spitting cobra is one time that wearing glasses is an advantage: spitting cobras appear to aim for the eyes, and the result is often blindness.

Because of these and other bizarre truths, snakes have more superstitions associated with them than any other group of animals. Many have been relegated to the realm of absurdity over the years, partly due to the higher levels of education in the United States. Few people believe anymore that snakes hypnotize people or roll down hills like hoops or that when a "glass snake" (actually a legless lizard) is hit it shatters into pieces that crawl back together after you leave. Those days of outlandish old wives' tales may be over, but some of the more plausible beliefs still are held and can be dismissed only by getting all of the facts. For example, rattlesnakes may shed their skins once or more than five times each year, attaining a new rattle segment each time. Obviously, then, a rattlesnake's age cannot be determined accurately by the number of rattles. The idea that cottonmouth moccasins do not open their mouths underwater and, therefore, cannot bite you also has a logical deductive step. That is, a main food in their diet is fish, a difficult food for them to catch alive without opening their mouths underwater. Actually, the dearth of underwater bites by cotton-mouths is more simply a consequence of their trying to escape rather than turn and bite if they are in the water.

Whether some snakes such as black mambas or king cobras actually will attack a person is not clearly resolved. But no U.S. snake routinely will do so. Despite what were once popular beliefs, racers and coachwhips almost invariably flee to the nearest hiding place when they see a human. However, many species including cottonmouths and several of the rattlesnakes indeed will stand their ground on certain occasions and not retreat. Therefore a person can be bitten if he or she does not see the snake.

One group of myths centers around how snakes administer their venom. No snake has a poisonous stinger, a trait reserved primarily for scorpions, stingrays, and certain insects, but some do have a sharp spine that forms the tip of the tail and that may be pressed against the skin when they are picked up. Likewise the forked tongue, as insidious as it may look, is only a sensory device used for collecting chemical information. No snake tongues are poisonous in any way. Although the saliva of some species may be mildly toxic, the only way snakes can deliver venom effectively is through their fangs.

Mothers often must be on the alert for the next pet that is brought home. Many have received the shock of hearing that it is—or, after an upper management decision, *was*—a snake. But many snakes are really not such bad choices as pets. How many guinea pigs or hamsters have to be fed and have their cages cleaned only once every two weeks? Snakes do not need exercise wheels, or daily walks, or rabies shots. In fact, most seem happy enough with a full water bowl and an old shoe box to hide under. Of course, poisonous snakes should never be kept as pets. In many communities laws have been passed to make it illegal to keep poisonous animals in the home.

Like most animals, the three thousand different kinds of snakes in the world come in all sizes. The tiniest are the blind snakes, species found throughout the warm regions of the world, including the southwestern United States. Some varieties attain a maximum size of less than six inches long and may weigh one-eighth of an ounce. Still in debate is what the largest snake ever caught was. The Atlanta Zoo cites a record of a thirty-seven-foot anaconda whereas the more usual records given in books and journals are of pythons and anacondas thirty-two to thirty-four feet long. Whatever the true record is, the giant snakes definitely can reach thirty-foot lengths. Most scientists regard any report of a snake more than forty feet long as a product of a superior imagination. The largest accepted records for U.S. snakes have been less than nine feet, although claims of larger specimens that were seen or killed, but never kept, continue to linger.

As rare as some seem to be, few snakes are offered governmental protection. Within the United States, the indigo snake, one of the most magnificent species in the Southeast, is an officially protected species in Florida, Georgia, and Alabama. Apparently requiring large tracts of undisturbed land for survival, the indigo snake has been seriously threatened by commercial land development throughout its range. In fact, this species already may have become extinct in South Carolina, where it was reported in the 1930s but whence no specimens have been recorded since. Snake species from other parts of the world receive limited forms of protection, too.

To be sure, snakes will continue to be killed unnecessarily by people who do not know better, because of fear and prejudice. However, nonpoisonous snakes create no problem for anyone. Even the poisonous varieties do not pose the threat with which they often are credited. Throughout the United States fewer than twenty snakebite deaths occur per year, although more than 2,000 people are bitten by poisonous snakes each year. Our worries in the United States are minimal, considering that as many as 10,000 people die each year from snakebites in other parts of the world. The U.S. figures for snakebite deaths are particularly insignificant when compared to the number of people killed each year in automobile accidents. Automobiles on a typical Labor Day weekend result in more human deaths in the United States than we experience in a quarter of a century from snakebites. Yet no one tries to eliminate Labor Day.

Snakes are an enigma, serving as living examples of species that people have tried to eradicate for centuries. Fortunately, the attempts have been unsuccessful in most instances although certain species still are thought to be coiled in the balance of survival or extinction.

CHAPTER 3

The Turtles:

Turtles May Be Slow but They're 200 Million Years Ahead of Us

The river water was rushing wildly past as we climbed into the twelve-foot pram. The consequence of pushing away from a river shore before you start your outboard motor is a lesson you are constantly retaught if you work around rivers. But that night I wasn't thinking when I pushed off. A remark from Don Tinkle at the stern of the boat gave evidence that he had not forgotten the lesson, and he wished I had not also. Fortunately, we finally did get the motor started, although half a mile of dark riverbank had passed by before we began moving upstream. The churning of the 5½-horsepower Evinrude was a welcome sound.

The White River in Arkansas seemed enormous to me that night. Wild. Even loud, until the motor started. A southern river at flood stage can become a fearful place if you think about the wrong things—such as having your small boat driven into a brush pile, overturned, and then being swept away yourself to wherever the river chooses to take you. We didn't wear life jackets or keep safety cushions in the 1950s and safety was some distance from our thoughts as we made our headway against the current. Turtles were all we really thought of as we edged our way back upstream to our starting point.

The occasional river spray over the bow was exhilarating. The mist looked silver in the backshine of my headlight as I swept the shoreline, looking for a good spot. I saw one and motioned for Tinkle to maneuver toward the bank. The shift in our angle to the current sent a splash over the port bow before we settled in to a steady movement toward the area where I pointed my light. The White River was up and angry from the heavy rains. I wondered if the technique would even work that night.

The river's rapid rate of flow actually helped our cause as we neared the brush pile. Using the handlebar-type accelerator, Tinkle powered down, let the boat drift backward, and then eased us up toward the tree limbs and bushes that were being buffeted by the strong current. I knelt on the cushion we kept in the bow and gripped the gunwales. My headlight scanned the bushes from a few inches above the surface down into the water itself.

When I saw the telltale yellow, the bright stripes on the dark green head, I shouted and pointed, keeping the light beam on the spot. The boat roared forward under full power, driving twigs and limbs against the sides of the boat and into my face and arms. But I got the turtle as it tried to dive beneath the submerged brush. I fell back into the boat. It was the first specimen I had ever seen of the Mississippi map turtle, with its owl-like yellow iris and shiny black pupil, so we drifted into a quiet indentation along the bank to take a look.

The technique for catching map turtles at night, as they sleep on brush piles in the river, was developed in the 1950s by herpetologists at Tulane University. During that decade the collecting method was tried on all of the major southern rivers by the Tulane field crews under the direction of Dr. Fred Cagle. Map turtles were collected by the thousands and found to be much more abundant than anyone had ever suspected. And each big river that drained into the Gulf of Mexico had its own prevalent species. The ringed sawback, a map turtle with spiny knobs down the center of a carapace adorned with a bright orange circle in each scale, was confined to the Pearl River of Louisiana and Mississippi. In the Pascagoula River lived the yellow-blotched sawback, a species that looked as if it had been splashed with gold paint; and the less colorful though handsomely ornamented black-knobbed sawback was endemic to the Warrior-Tombigbee drainages of Alabama. On the White River in Arkansas, our collection of thirty-eight turtles had added another river to the list of those where the Mississippi map turtle was known to occur.

The Tulane field crews established the map turtle–southern river relationship, described new species, revealed the abundance of others that were thought to be rare, and discovered that map turtles were restricted to the rivers in the gulf drainage. I intentionally have used the past tense about their distribution patterns.

One consequence of a major barge canal system to link the major southern rivers will be the destruction of the isolation enjoyed by the species endemic to particular river systems.

The collecting technique was exciting in several ways, for there are many biological adventures at night on the big southern rivers. The brush piles themselves serve as refuge for other animals besides turtles. Surface-swimming gar up to three or four feet long rest amid the underwater twigs. Water snakes and cottonmouth moccasins drape or coil through the upper branches. As many as a hundred of the vile-smelling, vicious (but nonpoisonous) diamond-back water snakes can be seen on the brush piles of an Alabama river on a good night.

An excitement comes with knowing that an endeavor has a certain real danger. On the river at night the dangers were usually obvious: the river itself, with its unawareness and lack of concern for your welfare; the occasional cottonmouth or, even more rarely, copperhead that had chosen to spend the night asleep on a limb amid the brush pile you charge into with a small boat. But the lesson of another danger was brought home to all river workers in the most dramatic way by Bob Webb on the Pearl River.

The brush pile where the real problem occurred was upstream from another one that Tinkle had had to back out of quickly. As the boat crept in from the main river channel, Webb's shout from the bow and frantic waving of his headlight revealed a large copper-head stretched along a head-high branch. Don Tinkle pulled the boat back into the safety of the river. A decision was made not to bother with any turtles that might have been in that brush pile, and the boat moved up to the next one. This time, Webb's hand motions gave evidence of turtles. The boat roared forward and Webb scrambled. He flipped a small ringed sawback turtle back into the middle of the boat and went after something else.

Legs kicking to keep himself in the boat, he grappled over the front end with something in the water. Then came the scream. Even the big bobcat that had been on the high bank half a mile downstream probably stopped dead still when he heard Bob Webb scream. Rather than fall back into the boat immediately, Webb continued to hang over the bow. Finally he rolled back onto the floor of the boat, and the problem was obvious. Attached to his Adam's apple was a large female slider turtle.

Bob had grabbed the big turtle in the brush pile, pulled her in toward the boat, and then got her too close to his neck. The turtle's grip was a solid one, deep into the flesh of his neck. And true to reputation, she was not letting go. In fact, ten minutes passed before Bob was free. A surgical operation at night on the Pearl River with only a greasy pair of pliers and a screwdriver takes time. Webb still has a scar on his neck, the turtle is permanently cataloged in the Tulane Museum Collection, and all of us now know to be extra careful when we lean over the front of a boat while catching turtles at night.

But all of us know beyond doubt that turtles are nowhere near "all bad" and scientists like myself are not the only ones who have an unmasked affection for these senior citizens of the reptile world. Turtles are like pet rocks that move. For some reason almost everyone likes them. Turtles are the only reptiles that automobile drivers will try not to hit. A mother who will accept no other wild pet often will tolerate a box turtle that is brought home for a visit. Several days later, she may even be the one who rescues it from behind the couch before releasing it into the backyard world. Why do so many people have such a warm fascination for these primitive reptiles?

I think it is because turtles possess traits we admire in ourselves and others—patience, perseverance, and the quality of being assertive without being too aggressive. Turtles are really tough, too. Many seem to be more resistant to various environmental abuses than are other vertebrates, having the ability to live in the chemically charged effluents from paper mills, coal-fired power plants, or other industries. Such environmental conditions may be completely inhospitable to fish and waterfowl. Turtles even have been found to be some of the most resistant animals in the world to radiation exposure. Turtles also are surprisingly rugged when it comes to accepting physical punishment such as from automobile and tractor tires, forest fires, and the assaults of predators like alligators, raccoons, and dogs. Although some do not make it, the tales of the scars and scrapes on the shells of the survivors would make true adventure stories.

The dinosaurs have set our image of reptiles as being big. And some of today's representatives have kept the tradition alive. People have nightmares about giant pythons of Africa, enormous man-eating crocodiles of New Guinea, and dinosaur-sized monitor lizards of Indonesia; but, paradoxically, the largest reptile in the world can occur naturally within view of the New York skyline. This modern-day leviathan, the leatherback sea turtle, roams the warm oceans of the world, nesting mainly on tropical beaches from Australia to the Americas. But its body size, which can approach a length of nine feet and a weight of one ton, provides a heat storage capacity that permits this most massive of today's reptiles to venture into the cold waters of the North Atlantic during the summer. None of the other sea turtles rivals the leatherback in size. In fact, this primitive species is believed to have such an ancient origin that its genealogical relationship to all other turtles is a biological mystery.

Although turtles ordinarily may not be thought of as being big, they traditionally are considered to be slow. Indeed land tortoises may possess the familiar turtle trait of slowness when they're racing rabbits. But don't sell all of the turtles short. Some of the marine and freshwater species can display remarkable speed underwater. For example, the so-called soft-shell turtles can outpace fish for short distances. These overgrown pancakes (many reach a diameter of two feet) have smooth, flat shells and huge webbed feet. The combination results in an impressive swimming machine that no human could keep up with underwater. However, the tales are true about the speed of turtles on land. For instance, the speed of a common box turtle in a hurry is so slow it cannot even travel a mile in four hours.

Turtle? Tortoise? Or terrapin? Which is what? Turtle terminology need not be confusing. All of them are turtles, whether they live in an ocean, desert, river, or pond. Today the term "tortoise" is sometimes confined to one family of turtles characterized by those from the Galápagos Islands. These species lead a completely terrestrial existence, a lifestyle enhanced by elephantine feet and large domed shells that permit storage of reserved fats and water. They eat primarily vegetation, a type of food even they can catch. The word "terrapin" also is taken by many to mean something unique, namely an edible turtle. In the early 1900s diamondback terrapins from Chesapeake Bay and other coastal waters were judged to be a gourmet's prize. Raising them in experimental turtle farms along the Atlantic Coast, the U.S. Bureau of Commercial Fisheries spent a wealth of research money to understand the biology of these animals. So today some may think of "terrapin" as having special meaning. But to the Algonquin Indians, from whom the word originated, a terrapin was any kind of turtle.

Having grown up with an awareness of turtle soup and dime-store hatchlings and having had frequent highway encounters with ambling box turtles, most U.S. citizens take turtles for granted. Few realize that eastern North America, along with Southeast Asia, has more than two continents' share of turtles. For example, fewer than half a dozen species occur in Europe whereas the state of Florida alone has twenty-three kinds of terrestrial and fresh-water turtles, not to mention five species of sea turtles that have been known to nest on Florida beaches. Even all of Australia with its almost five hundred kinds of lizards and snakes has only nineteen species of turtles. South America and Africa fare better with approximately thirty-five species each, slightly fewer than the number found in the eastern United States. But do not take the commonness of turtles too lightly. Some of them could be in danger.

Turtles, like many other groups of animals, have found their way into the legally threatened or endangered species ranks. Many of the threats could be serious indeed. The loggerhead sea turtle is a recent arrival to the list prepared by the Endangered Species Section of the U.S. Fish and Wildlife Service. In the United States, loggerheads nest on southern beaches. A female can nest more than five times in a summer, laying over a hundred ping pong ball–looking eggs each time. How can there be any danger of extinction for such a prolific creature? Take a look at what's happening to the beaches of the Gulf of Mexico and the Atlantic Ocean and you will understand. Coastal development, too often with an eye for profit, is diminishing the effective nesting area of these and other sea turtles. We must be cautious lest we develop the passenger pigeon syndrome that befell our great-grandparents—that is, the error of believing that an abundant species is not one we have to worry about protecting.

The seven kinds of sea turtles that exist today inhabit all of the major oceans of the world. In the United States sea turtles nest from March to August. Loggerheads nest on beaches of the gulf and along the Atlantic coast as far north as Virginia. The green sea turtle and a few others nest primarily along the Florida coastline. Although most species also inhabit the Pacific waters, nesting occurs only as far north as Mexico. The life cycle of sea turtles is fascinating from the standpoint of their dependence upon land. Were it not for a need to nest on a beach, sea turtles probably would be no worse off today than most other ocean animals. After about sixty days of incubation and a few more of scrambling around in the nest and digging out, the young scamper to the surf and enter the ocean environment. For most males this ocean life is forever. For the females it is until their first eggs are laid, many years later. A baby sea turtle successfully hatching from its egg still must survive several years in the ocean before reaching maturity. No one knows exactly where baby sea turtles spend their time, but we do know that they must face numerous hardships and dangers, such as seabirds, sharks, and the nets of shrimp trawlers. Scientists estimate that as few as one in five thousand survive to breeding age. So, despite remarkably high egg numbers, the sea turtles justifiably can be considered as endangered species.

Can turtles be dangerous? Some can, to be sure. The common snapping turtle is perhaps the most cosmopolitan of the true grouches of the turtle world, ranging throughout most of the United States and southern Canada down to Mexico and into Central America. Snappers often are encountered on land, a place where they feel insecure and act in a very hostile manner to intruders. A big snapping turtle of twenty-five to thirty pounds unquestionably would leave a V-shaped scar if it got you on a soft spot. Or, it possibly could crack a finger or a foot bone. However, stories of broken broom handles are probably only legend. Another species, the gargantuan alligator snapper of the Mississippi River Valley, with specimens on record of more than one hundred pounds, and with a mouth that opens wider than a steel mammal trap, could do untold damage to any part of a person it grabbed. Fortunately alligator snappers usually stay in the water and actually use their tongues, pink and wiggling, to lure hungry fish into their open mouths. Violence is not the style of most turtles, although many will nip you if you trespass too far. In contrast, some species, such as the docile Blanding's turtle of the Midwest, never try to bite humans at all.

The alligator snapping turtle of the Mississippi Valley is one of the largest freshwater species in the world. Many specimens attain sizes of more than one hundred pounds. An alligator snapper lies in the water with its huge mouth open and wiggles its pink, fleshy tongue, which resembles an earthworm. Fish attracted to the "bait" become an instant meal when the open jaws slam shut.

Everyone knows you can eat turtles, but did you know there are some you had better not eat? The common box turtle is one such variety, and the reason is pretty simple. You could die from the experience if the box turtle has dined recently on poisonous mushrooms. Certain deadly chemicals that apparently do not faze the box turtle presumably can be incorporated temporarily into muscle tissue in an unaltered state. Hence, to eat the box turtle might differ little from consuming the toadstool itself. On rare occasions similar situations have been known to occur with sea turtles. One medical case involved severe poisoning deaths of two dozen persons. The culprit was a hawksbill sea turtle that formed the basis for the chef's soup. Unfortunately, the turtle recently had fed on a form of seaweed that does no harm to a turtle but is toxic to humans. But these are the exceptions. The large aquatic species in this country, including snappers, soft shells, and the common slider and painted turtles, are as edible as chicken though much harder to cut open and clean.

Are turtles important ecologically? Unquestionably so in some regions. For instance, turtles have an environmental impact on more bodies of water in the South than do fish. The reason is simple: turtles can live not only in permanent lakes and reservoirs but also in shallow water depressions or roadside ditches that dry up during parts of the year. More than twenty-five kinds of freshwater turtles can be found in the Southeast. The most common of these is the yellow-bellied slider turtle. In fact, this turtle is probably the one reptile that nearly every Southerner has seen in its natural habitat at one time or another. In the Midwest and along the eastern seaboard, the slider is replaced by the common painted turtle, which seems to abound any place that stays wet for more than a few days a year. These turtles are usually among the species you see basking on logs in most freshwater habitats.

How do turtles manage to survive so well? For one thing, ecological studies show that slider turtles will eat anything they can catch, including plant materials, seeds, dead fish, and insects. And, incidentally, there is no evidence that they successfully can catch living game fish of any sort although they probably eat more noxious algae in a lifetime than do most of our native fishes. Aside from their dietary indiscretion, another reason for the ubiquity of aquatic turtles is their remarkable ability to be either aquatic or

Baby eastern mud turtles spend most of their first year of life underground. Females dig a nest and lay two to five hard-shelled eggs in the spring. The eggs hatch about three months later, but the babies remain in the nest through the fall and winter. The following spring they emerge from the ground and go to the nearest body of water.

terrestrial, whichever suits the conditions. As many as half of the turtles in a lake venture onto land each year for purposes other than egg laying. Some of the terrestrial activity of the adult males can be ascribed to travel from one lake to another, perhaps in search of mates or food sources. However, sometimes a turtle may leave a lake for a few hours or days and then return to the same place. Whatever the reasons, aquatic turtles have the ability to travel overland and can thus vacate an undesirable habitat. Clearly this trait is a valuable survival tactic for any animal and probably, coupled with the ever-present suit of armor, is one reason that allows such an ancient animal to survive in a modern, rapidly changing world.

A final trait of turtles that causes them to be held in awe by humans is that some do live for many years. Authentic records exist

Turtles provide an investigator with the advantage of being able to recognize particular individuals throughout their entire life (which may be up to thirty years) by drilling holes in the scutes of the shell. Various identification codes can be used so that each turtle has its own number. The holes do not injure the turtle in any way, are permanent, and permit individuals to be recognized after several years. A portable drill permits researchers to mark animals in the field and release them at the site of capture.

for several species that indicate some specimens have lived for more than half a century. Although the longevity of turtles is legendary, little documentation is available to show that many live more than seventy-five years. Although an age of fifty to seventy-five years is impressive and is a much longer lifespan than most animals have, scientific evidence of particular turtles living for one hundred years appears to be lacking. Turtles indeed may hold longevity records of a century or more and frequent newspaper assertions have been made regarding such records, but scientists do not really know how long the oldest turtles live.

Turtles serve as an example of the paradox we see in modern environmental science. That is, we can overwhelm ourselves with how much we know about one facet of a subject whereas our depth of understanding about another aspect may be far short of impressive. This paradox is the state of ecology today and is where all ecologists find themselves within their own research and training. A vast foundation of ecological knowledge and expertise has been successfully developed that is applicable to furthering the development of basic research and, in some instances, for solving practical (which means human and immediate) problems. But the blocks needed to build this foundation must be formed with great toil and placed with utmost care.

One example of the role that turtles have played in understanding how particular environmental systems function is the one of AL. I knew that AL was the biggest yellow-bellied slider turtle I had ever seen when personnel from DuPont's health physics division walked in the door with it on April Fool's Day, 1968. A freak, I thought. An anomaly that we coded "AL," using our personal identification scheme in which we clipped or drilled holes in the marginal scutes of a turtle's shell in a pattern that distinguished it from all others in the population. After coding it "AL," we released it back into Par Pond, the site of capture. We had captured more than three hundred slider turtles on the SRP in the previous year, and I had read every scientific paper written about the species. The largest one ever reported from the United States was about ten inches long. This one from Par Pond was more than a foot in total length and weighed six and a half pounds. The maximum we had previously recorded was only four pounds. This turtle was definitely different and we wanted to know why. The routine monitoring program of DuPont's health physics division had provided me with a biological mystery.

During my first year at SREL I had stayed clear of the mysterious thermal reservoir with its rising mists and lukewarm temperatures in the dead of winter. I suppose any biologist would assume things were different on such a lake. We knew there were no snakes but lots of alligators; and we knew something about the fish, from tales and experience; but we knew nothing about the turtles. After seeing and measuring AL, I redirected our turtle trapping from two Carolina bays to Par Pond. If the ecology was that different, we simply had to know more.

The SRP is a big place (1 percent of the size of South Carolina) to be a protected area, and our lab was small—half a dozen scientists, all young. The area averaged out to fifty square miles apiece, an area covering a greater diversity of habitats and environmental interactions than could be thoroughly studied by all the ecologists at a large university in a decade. So, I was not feeling guilty about not having examined the situation at Par Pond in lieu of having been involved in numerous other endeavors. But AL was too much. The explanation for a turtle specimen that was bigger than any known for the species outside the tropics had to be pursued.

We had set out in the SREL boat in search of a place to put traps, but our first job had been to get some bait. We used largemouth bass—fresh bass that we could catch a few minutes after shoving off from shore. The Par Pond bass population is now legendary, and we already knew about that feature from previous experience along the shoreline of the lake.

Sitting in the boat amid the shifting curtains of fog, we cast twenty times and caught twelve bass, each over two and a half pounds. We had taken the boat to the area known as the "boil" or the "bubble-up" or the "hot dam," where the heated water entered Par Pond from a 300-acre holding pond that I was soon to name "Pond Classified," to subtly show my annoyance at not being allowed to take the temperatures because of defense security reasons. But that's another story. The water entered through a large, rock-filled culvert that ran from "Pond C," as it eventually was called, under the SRP highway, and connected Par Pond with the holding pond. When you sat quietly in the boat you could hear the gurgling water as the warm effluent bubbled up and mixed with the cool natural waters of the reservoir. We caught our bait there in ten minutes and headed out to find a suitable place to set the traps. Setting the traps in the misty, warm end of the reservoir was no problem as we simply put them at fifty-foot intervals along the sparsely vegetated shoreline. Then we set out to find a spot to set traps in the unheated parts of the lake.

As the boat slipped out into the open water, toward the cooler part of the lake, the fog thinned and we could see the brilliant blue of the early April sky. The final shreds of mist were left behind. The wind on my face was cool, and as I unbuttoned my shirt and let it blow in the breeze I could feel the penetrating warmth of the sun's rays. When we came upon a dozen or so coots dipping and diving near one shore, the small flock responded to our rapid approach in their characteristic manner. Going in different directions, they dispersed out of the boat's path. Frantically flapping their short wings and using their big blue webbed feet to run on the surface, they flopped across the water like a flock of black chickens with white bills. One of them had been caught completely off guard and tried to escape in the same direction our boat was traveling. Realizing its folly, the fat water bird plunged beneath the surface in front of the approaching bow. The absurd creature surfaced in our wake and fled to the sanctuary of the nearest cattail stand.

The water looked like a blue mirror as we sped along, taking the west arm of the reservoir when we came to the major fork. Selecting the first big cove, whence AL had come, we turned into it. Cutting the outboard motor to near-idling speed we drifted slowly into the area, through the young shoots of the season's first lily pads. Sparse and fragile, they offered no resistance at this time of year. Later in the spring and summer, with their tough, fibrous stems, they would be a scourge to any propeller and receive innumerable curses from ecologists, including us, in years to come. Having had no experience with trapping in the reservoir, we could only guess about where to put the two traps we had left, but we set them in the large cove, each one baited with a beheaded largemouth bass.

As we rode back across the lake, having released AL, I could not recall ever having been so anticipatory about what we might catch in a turtle trap. I thought of AL and marveled at its size, wondering if it were the exception or the rule in Par Pond. I considered an explanation involving in some way the heated waters and the fact that a reptile might be able to stay active longer during fall and winter than would be normal and therefore have opportunity to eat more. The disquieting part of that hypothesis was that AL had been collected in a cove where water temperatures did not seem appreciably higher than natural waters of the region. Of course, one hypothesis might be that AL had actually come *from* the warm end of the lake and that the turtles lived there in an active feeding-state year round rather than going through the four or five months of winter dormancy characteristic of the turtles in natural lakes in South Carolina.

The next day we learned a lot about turtles and turtle trapping in Par Pond. The first lesson came at the warm end of the lake where we had set six hoop traps and had made the serious mistake of not tying them with rope to anything on shore. The warm end of Par Pond is shallow along much of the shore, so we had placed the traps in foot-deep water. Because they were on a level bottom, I had seen no need to anchor them. The first two traps were gone and could not be found. The third trap was collapsed and lying out in water about three feet deep. I pulled the trap from the bottom and was impressed. Something had pretzeled two of the quarter-inch-diameter steel hoops. They were bent beyond easy repair and the heavy netting had an eighteen-inch gash on one side. The largemouth bass used for bait was gone. One of the next three traps also was bent and the others were moved but unharmed. None of the bait was to be found in the traps, nor were any turtles. But obviously the bait had worked for something.

At that time we were not aware that many of the Par Pond alligators reach lengths of ten to twelve feet and that alligators show no respect for research plans. We also were not aware that because alligators are primarily nocturnal feeders we would not be able to leave our traps in overnight without risking trap destruction. The Carolina bays and farm ponds in which we had worked heretofore had either small alligators or none at all. The small ones got caught right along with the turtles. As we started toward AL's cove, I was pensive, as well as annoyed, about the results so far. Not only had we learned nothing about the turtles in Par Pond, we had lost four of our six turtle traps.

As we entered AL's cove I was gratified to see the top part of the hoops of both traps. At least they were not lost or destroyed. We drifted toward the nearest trap and our excitement rose when the hoops began to vibrate in the water. We definitely had caught something! I pulled the trap over the side of the boat and felt as close as a field ecologist can get to saying "Eureka!" The trap held three enormous yellow-bellied slider turtles as big as AL plus two others that were about the size of adult females from natural habitats of the region. So, AL was not a freak. Something was really happening at an environmental level. Also, the two smallest turtles in the trap proved interesting in a different manner. Rather than being the eight- or ten-year-old specimens that would be expected for the size category, both animals were judged to be only four years old on the basis of the easily visible scute annuli. Their rate of growth was phenomenal! The most parsimonious explanation of those incipient observations on the turtles in Par Pond was that somehow the elevated water temperatures had created a unique ecological situation that resulted in rapid growth and large body size in at least one species of freshwater turtle.

Our understanding of the phenomenon became further enlightened in 1973 when we discovered a population of yellow-bellied slider turtles on Kiawah Island near Charleston, South Carolina. Although ecologists were aware that giant loggerhead sea turtles lumber onto Kiawah's beaches each year to lay eggs, no one had suspected that the freshwater turtles inhabiting the barrier island would prove to be the largest of their kind. In the spring of 1973 we caught several specimens as big or bigger than AL. Kiawah Island's turtles were ecologically similar to those in Par Pond. Somehow the island's natural environment, presumably because of warm water temperatures and a rich food supply, had the same effect on growth and size of turtles as did the artificial reservoir system on the SRP. Ironically, the heated water environments on the SRP had made us aware of a phenomenon that proved to occur in natural environments such as Kiawah Island.

Whether a person is an ecologist, an environmentalist, or neither, one wants electricity, and a frequent by-product of its production is heated water. We can expect these resulting thermal elevations of aquatic environments to alter certain plant and animal relationships—slightly in some instances, greatly in others. One role of the ecologist is to establish general principles of how organisms, reptiles and amphibians in my case, respond to these thermal changes so that biological outcomes can be predicted and the most satisfactory balance can be achieved between economic and environmental considerations.

Many avenues have yet to be pursued to complete our understanding of how heated water influences and controls biological systems. However, enough is now known, partly on the basis of research with turtles, to state that thermal effects cannot be categorically classed as detrimental or beneficial. Because thermal alteration affects aquatic communities indirectly and subtly, as well as in a direct and forceful manner, long periods of time may be required before proper documentation is available. Establishing whether an impact is detrimental, beneficial, or neutral is dependent upon which environmental components or species populations receive the emphasis and upon our social and economic value system.

To the general public the visibility and/or importance of the particular community feature or species will determine the emphasis it receives. The ecological value—that is, the importance of the species or the environmental feature to the functioning of the particular ecosystem—also will enter into the decision when such information is available. Providing this information is the responsibility of the ecologist, and for a herpetologist like me turtles are one way to set about doing so.

CHAPTER 4

The Crocodilians:

How to Catch an Alligator in
One Uneasy Lesson

"You know," I said with seeming casualness, "we could run across an alligator at Steed Pond."

"Oh yeah," said Morton, suspicion creeping into his voice. Apparently his first day as my technician at the Savannah River Ecology Laboratory was turning out differently than he had expected. Most technicians wear white lab coats, sit on tall stools, and write on clipboards. Here he sat bouncing down a dirt road in an old pickup truck, wearing a pair of muddy hip boots, and carrying a plastic sack full of fish heads. The fish were to be used to rebait turtle traps as part of my research program.

"What then?" he asked, almost antagonistically. I looked at him disapprovingly. He began to shrug his shoulders and rephrase. "Well, I mean, what are we going to do if we find one?"

I answered with a touch of incredulity. "We're going to catch and measure it. Research, you know. Besides," I added, "it would be the first one I've ever seen in the wild."

"Oh," said Morton. He turned to stare out the window. Morton obviously did not wish to pursue a discussion on the justification for catching and measuring an alligator, even if it were your first one.

I stopped the Dodge pickup at a pullover about fifty yards from Steed Pond. We left our shirts in the truck and carried the fish heads with us down the brier-lined path. When we stood above the muddy bank that sloped steeply down to the water, I surveyed the lake.

"Hey, I thought a trap was set right along here," I motioned downward with a hand wave. "In fact, I remember holding on to this stump to get out of the water. It looks like something pulled the trap away from shore, out toward the middle."

"Yeah," said Morton, with a concerned glance toward me.

"I'll go get it. You check and rebait the one over there near the shore." I held on to the stump and slid down the muddy slope.

The water in Steed Pond is relatively clear and less than knee deep for the most part. But the loose silt bottom is generally at least a foot thick and walking in the pond is like wading in a huge bowl of oatmeal with a topping of milk.

As I slogged through the muck toward the displaced trap, Morton moved along shore toward the other one. My feet kicked up brown, swirling clouds in the clear water as they moved beneath the layer of silt. Steed Pond contains no logs or other debris so I was not really concerned about stumbling.

I turned to watch Morton as I walked along. He lifted the net trap out of the water and I saw two large turtles. I yelled to ask what kind they were. His answer was obliterated by my second yell as I fell over a large log that I knew should not be there.

"It's an alligator!" I remarked at the top of my lungs. And, in a wide-awake nightmare, I could not pick up my feet to run. When I jerked upward with one foot the other one went deep into the mud. I prepared myself, as best one can, to be devoured, forgetting for the moment that I could leave in the same fashion as I had gotten there.

But, upon reconsideration, I did not need to leave, for the big animal was apparently afraid of me. A strange courage came over me as the alligator began to swim slowly away. Suddenly, I wanted it to stay. Like most herpetologists I had always wanted to catch the king of American reptiles. At last I was face to face with my first one, and I did not want it to escape.

"Hey, Morton, he's moved away but he's just burying under the silt layer where he thinks I can't see him. Let's catch him. Run back and get that bunch of nylon rope in the back of the truck. We can lasso him."

Morton left the sack of fish heads on the bank and disappeared into the brush. I turned to watch the big layer of silt that thought it was invisible, as it lay completely motionless on the bottom. Morton returned, breathless. He began wadding the tangled rope into a ball to throw.

"Hey," I said, "don't throw it. Just wade out here and give it to me. Besides, you do want to see him, don't you?"

"Yeah," grumbled Morton. He reluctantly entered the water and from a few feet away pitched me the raveled pink rope. After finding one end, I made an extra big noose and prepared for the test. Approaching within inches of the big animal's tail, I sighted the large snout several feet away. With a lump in my throat I tossed the loop end, leaving the remainder of the rope draped over my arms and shoulders.

The top of the nylon lasso splashed into the water just in front of the animal's snout; the loop sank slowly, tilted at an angle, encircling the front half of the alligator. Then the alligator began to move. The huge tail stirred up a cloud of mud in front of me. Steed Pond's leviathan began to swim away. And, by good fortune it moved snout first, right through the center of the lasso.

Most people plan no course of action for an event they never expect to happen. So I am probably with the majority who have really given only passing thought, at best, to what they would do upon finding themselves standing knee deep in a muddy lake tangled up in a piece of pink nylon rope with a full-grown American alligator attached to the other end. All I knew for sure was that whatever happened we must not lose the gator. Thinking back, I apparently also had been holding certain reservations about being towed around Steed Pond by an alligator, because with uncanny speed and agility I slipped free of the snarl of rope and threw the whole mess to Morton, who was watching entranced from the edge of the water.

"Run," I yelled at his back. "Tie the rope around that stump before he gets away." I could just as well have been talking to the gator, for Morton was obviously the one getting away at this point, and without undue ceremony. The bulk of the rope had gone over Morton's head, settled on his shoulders, and segments were trailing along behind him as he left the water at full gallop.

But the slippery bank was not to be scaled so easily, especially when Morton stepped on the plastic bag full of fish heads. He thrashed and floundered on the muddy bank like a catfish out of water. Mud, pink nylon rope, and fish heads were flying everywhere. Meanwhile the alligator had picked up speed and was heading away from shore.

"Get the rope around that stump," I shouted. "He's going out to the middle." The slack between the alligator's neck and Morton's was rapidly being taken up as the monster moved away.

Morton was only mildly frantic amid the snarl of rope as he lunged for the stump at the top of the slope. He caught it and dragged himself up the muddy bank. Then, as the slack was running out, Morton looped part of the rope twice around the stump and began to unravel himself from the remainder. The section of rope between stump and gator went taut.

I've seen many a big fish jump impressively after being hooked. But an adult alligator reaching the end of its rope is a fantastic spectacle! That dark-green monster's snout came at least five feet out of the lake while its tail churned the shallow water into a froth. When the animal landed, muddy water splashed all over me, which brought me to the sobering realization that I was standing in the water beside a not-so-calm alligator.

"Sorry," I said to Morton, two seconds later as I clambered over his body at the water's edge and pushed myself up to the stump. "Didn't mean to pull you in, but I couldn't get a handhold. Here." I graciously extended my hand down to him.

We dripped in silence on the bank as our catch swam in an arc at the end of the rope.

"That was easy enough," I said. Morton gave me a strange look. "Now all we have to do is haul him in and take him back to the lab." Morton made a peculiar sound in his throat.

I began pulling the animal in a foot at a time and looping the slack over the stump.

"Hey, man, look at that mouth," said Morton, as we finally got our catch to the water's edge. "And his tail. Isn't an alligator's tail pretty dangerous, too?"

"Only if you get in the way," I said, trying to look smug and sound clever. "I wonder what we should do now."

After answering Morton's suggestion by reminding him we had already eaten lunch, I motioned for him to help me. We began to tug on the rope, gradually moving the gator's head out of the water and up the muddy slope. When we had pulled the animal so that the forelegs were beginning to clear the water I made a loop in the free end of the rope and slipped it over the broad snout.

The alligator had been placid since reaching shore and remained so as I tightened the snout noose. I held on to the stump, leaned down, and took several half-hitches around the snout with the rope. The potentially dangerous jaws were now harmless. I chose this moment as a proper point to play teacher with Morton.

"That stuff you've heard about alligators having weak jaws when it comes to opening them is true," I said, with the bored air that implies long experience. "In fact, you see how his mouth is a little bit open right now, 'cause the ropes are too loose? I'll hold his jaws shut with one hand while you tighten the loops."

I knelt down to the now helpless creature and reached for the trussed-up snout. The jaws were parted about one inch. I put my right thumb on the gator's nose and my fingers under its chin. I was exceedingly glad to find I had told Morton the truth. The animal was obviously powerless, at least in regard to opening its jaws. I actually held them shut with one hand.

Morton, seeing the ease with which I held the mouth shut, leaned down to help. He began to pull the loops tighter around the big jaws. The alligator, half out of the water, lay quietly and watched, probably in amazement, as two mortals continued to truss up its snout. Before Morton could finish the job, however, we learned the second part of the jaw-holding lesson that nobody ever tells you.

The lesson: if you ever hold an alligator's mouth shut with one hand, something a child could do, you had better make sure that the rest of the animal is in a vise. Because there is a point at which an alligator becomes unhappy about someone holding its mouth shut and it begins to twist. Fast. And it rolls over and over. And the person holding the jaws shut also rolls over and over. As does anyone in the process of tightening pink nylon rope around the snout. And when all this happens on a slippery mud bank beside a lake, the outcome is inevitable.

"Get out of the way of his tail," I yelled when I surfaced. I repeated the suggestion when Morton finally came up, practically beneath me. The monster was spinning around and around on the mud, its tail slapping the water right in front of us as we stood waist deep in the hole. It seemed somewhat angry about the whole situation. Indifference would hardly describe Morton's and my emotions, either.

We both lunged for the nearest shoreline vegetation to pull ourselves out of the lake. Using vegetation to pull oneself out of the water is not unusual, although ordinarily we would not choose blackberry bushes with briers. By the time we had reached the top of the bank and extracted the thorns from our hands, arms, and faces, the alligator had stopped turning over. It was now two feet farther up the slope due to the twisting of the rope between its neck and the stump. The animal lay on its belly peering up at us, waiting for our next move. We peered down, waiting for its.

"All right now," I said at last, "let's get that loop back around his snout and get him out." Morton rolled his eyes skyward.

We repeated the snout noose process but this time we decided the loops were tight enough even though the alligator could open its mouth an inch or so.

"What do we do now?" asked Morton, cocking his head down and sort of looking up at me. He obviously would be pleased to learn we were now going to release our prey by cutting the rope.

"What do you mean?" I asked. "We're going to put him in the truck. Let's just lift the rope off the stump and pick him up."

Interestingly enough, as formidable as an alligator is at either end, the limbs are essentially harmless. The relatively small legs are fleshy and limp and the claws are practically useless. The legs do make good handles, though, when carrying a sizable gator. We each picked up a front leg, put one arm under the chest, and let the tail drag along, several feet behind. We actually went the 150 feet to the truck without incident.

When we reached the pickup, Morton let the tailgate down and we pushed the animal in head first. In went the snout and the front legs. Then we each reached for a back leg as a handhold to shove the rest of the creature in. As I remember it, the realization that Morton and I were prime targets for the long tail struck me about the same time that that monstrous tail did. Two swishes sent Morton hurtling backward into the blackberry bushes (with briers) on one side of the road and me into those on the other. Our captive did not move from the truck bed while Morton and I compared bruised rib cages and picked thorns out of each other's backs.

We brought up the tailgate, enclosing the alligator in the back of the truck. "Okay," I said, "we've got to fix it some way so that he can't get out while we drive to the lab. It seems to me that the only way we can really be sure he stays back here is to put the rope through the cab with both ends tied around his neck. That way he can't climb out over the side."

Morton gave me another strange look, sideways this time, and asked, "How are we going to get in the truck? The doors will be tied shut."

"The windows," I said. "We can climb through the windows." I gingerly removed the snarl of rope by cutting it up near the snout. I left the noose around the alligator's neck and threw the rope in one window and out the other. I tied the other end around the gator's neck after removing the slack. Because the doors were now held shut, we crawled through our respective windows. Ready at last to bring the vanquished foe home, we started down the bumpy dirt road toward the highway leading to the lab.

We both had to lean forward because the rope passing through the cab was touching the backs of our necks. When Morton muttered something about the tangle of rope, I thought about the small knot in the rope behind my right ear. What bothered me, as we were streaking down the highway, was that the knot had been behind my left ear when we started. The knot suddenly slid over another foot or so into the middle of the cab.

Startled by the sudden rope burn on the back of his neck, Morton jerked forward too quickly and bumped his forehead on the metal dashboard. Without a break in rhythm, he rebounded to the back window and peered out.

"Oh my God," he shrieked, eyes wider than ever. "He's got the rope off his nose and he's moving toward your window!"

I had never found myself driving a pickup with the doors tied shut and a full-grown alligator coming in the window, so I hesitated momentarily about what do do. One inclination was to stop, bail out the other window, and run for my life. This notion was strongly and loudly supported by Morton. But I would not be robbed of victory so close to the laboratory. I rammed the gas pedal to the floor.

Minutes later I skidded the gray Dodge pickup truck into the laboratory parking lot, stopped abruptly, and, mud-covered and wet, Morton and I emerged together through one window while the large alligator entered through the other. Both nooses were still intact around its neck, but its jaws seemed to be working quite well. Once outside, Morton and I stared at the spectacle of the head partially inside the cab, the large body curving around on the outside, and the tail resting in the truck bed.

"Boy, is he mad," I said.

"Yeah," said Morton.

As we stood there, word of the captive spread through the laboratory. This animal was the first sizable alligator to be brought in and soon more than a dozen secretaries, technicians, and graduate students stood watching. Morton and I tried to look casual as we answered the salvo of questions about the capture.

Finally, I said, "Well, let's get him measured and tagged. We need to take him back to the lake this afternoon. I guess the first thing to do is get his jaws tied shut again."

In the next few minutes we safely managed to tie up the alligator and measure its eight-foot, four-inch body from snout to tip of tail. We then carried it into the lab building to be tagged for future identification. The scene reminded me of a primitive tribe as we moved across the lawn. Morton and I held the front legs, two graduate students the back. The other males in the group formed a small cluster around the captive while the secretaries and female technicians followed a few feet behind in a compact, chattering huddle. The image was completed by two graduate students who had picked up pieces of aluminum conduit from the truck bed and were carrying them over their shoulders, like spears. The procession moved into the building.

Ten minutes later we emerged. Without mishap, a metal identification tag normally used for large mammals had been placed through one of the finlike scales along the top of the tail. The alligator now could be referred to as Number 38-1.

As we carried the animal back to the truck, someone suggested we untie it and put it on the ground "to see what he will do." We put it down on the lawn and I removed the pink rope from the snout and limbs. Its first response was to open its mouth slightly and hiss, loudly. The gator lay there with its mouth open, looking rather angry and not particularly vanquished. The situation seemed perfect for finding out if alligator jaws are as powerful as generally believed.

A graduate student, in the true spirit of exploring the unknown, began to poke old 38-1 on the top of the snout with a piece of hollow aluminum conduit. Comment ran through the crowd that maybe we should "let him bite the conduit to see if he'll scratch, or even dent it." The student moved the pipe end down alongside the animal's mouth with the intent of further teasing before letting it bite.

No chance! The alligator's head snapped to the side, grabbed the pipe, and whipped back to the other side so fast that the student could not even release his grip before he was pulled into the arena himself. And then, with a screaming graduate student across its back and surrounded by an audience aghast, the alligator swung its head sharply back and released the pipe. The whirring of the pipe passing overhead and the crash as it went through a window added to the air-raid atmosphere. This whiplash was followed by 38-1's demonstration of how fast big alligators can run on land. About all I can say, biologically, is that they do not move faster than secretaries, technicians, graduate students, or research ecologists.

Morton and I ended up in the ladies' rest room, where the pipe had gone, so we looked to see if the alligator had scarred it. My respect for the species grew when I saw the two holes, almost a foot apart, which went through one side and came out the other.

"Got quite a bite," I noted.

"Yeah," said Morton.

After regrouping and assessing the situation, we recaptured our captive before it scored another victory. Properly tied up, the alligator was escorted back to Steed Pond by me, Morton, and two graduate students. We carried the animal to the water's edge, put its snout in the water, and undid the knots.

I jerked the rope off and jumped back along the shore. The gator looked around and for an instant I thought it might decide it had a little unfinished business on shore. But my intuition was right. Having touched the water, 38-1 knew it was home. And with a most graceful movement the animal entered with hardly a splash. A swish of the huge tail sped it faster than a fish toward the center of the lake. A ways out from shore the gator stopped and turned sideways, watching us. Then its head turned quickly away and went underwater. Our last sight of the big beast was the huge wave created by its tail in this final submergence, a disdainful parting comment to the insignificant beings who clearly belonged to a race of evolutionary afterthoughts.

Perhaps the most remarkable group of U.S. animals from the standpoint of limited research emphasis versus high public visibility are the two crocodilian species native to North America.

Although the American crocodile seems headed for extinction, American alligators are again a dominant feature of the Southeast, and although millions were exterminated by hide seekers during the past forty years, the endangered species laws now protect them to some degree.

The American alligator and the American crocodile (whose final haunts in the United States are restricted to brackish habitats in southern Florida) both enjoy endangered species status throughout much of the Southeast. The penalty for "pursuing, harming, hunting, trapping, killing," or even "harassing" an endangered species in the United States can be up to $20,000 and two years in jail. This concern for the fewer than two dozen crocodilian species remaining in the world today is not restricted to the United States. Even the dreaded Nile crocodile of Africa, one of the few species of animals left on earth that will attack a full-grown human for food, is protected. Importation of their skins into the United States is illegal.

The American alligator is one of the two species of modern crocodilians that range into the temperate zone. In fact, the other species, the Chinese alligator, may be extinct in the wild with the last survivors being a handful of zoo animals.

People in southern states, particularly Louisiana and Florida, express wonder at the protection of the American alligator because they now appear to be abundant in many areas. Once again they can be found in every coastal state from Texas to North Carolina. But how abundant were they only a decade or so ago in areas where alligator poachers, or "caimaneros," had made their claims? Not very. At night, an unsuspecting, previously undisturbed population of alligators could be approached one at a time and hit in the head with an axe. A seven-foot-long slow learner made a handsome pelt and a lot of shoes. Two-foot-long juveniles were even more abundant and easier to kill and handle: so no animals were spared.

Thus, alligators can practically disappear from a region after a successful assault by the hide-seeking caimaneros. The current legal protection offers the American alligator a chance to regain the status it enjoyed in the 1700s when William Bartram of the American Philosophical Society reported seeing alligators in nearly unbelievable numbers in some of the southern rivers.

Our American alligator's closest relative is (or was) the Chinese alligator, now represented by a few scattered individuals in the zoos of the world. Although possibly extinct now in its native habitats in the Yangtze River drainage, Chinese alligator hides were sold on the world market in the late 1950s. The young of the two species are indistinguishable by the casual observer; however, the adults of the Oriental species seldom reach more than six or eight feet in length, whereas most southern states can boast of American alligators over eleven or twelve feet long. Alligator length records of over fifteen feet have been documented in the United States and a nineteen-foot specimen from Louisiana has been sworn upon but not measured. So, who knows how long the biggest one ever was or, maybe now, will be?

To the scientist, alligators are an ecological paradox. The largest, most apparent aquatic reptile in the South should have been studied extensively by ecologists. Yet until recently the rarity of alligators prevented this research. Hence, few major studies have been conducted on the ecology of the American alligator and, with few exceptions, detailed, carefully documented information has appeared in the scientific literature only in recent years.

All crocodilians in the world lay eggs, and alligators lay theirs in the springtime or early summer. The female builds a large, often extraordinarily well-concealed nest of mud and debris along shore and deposits the twenty to sixty eggs in the center of the mound. The young hatch in the late summer or fall and enter the water at that time or in the following spring. Recent evidence indicates that the females of some crocodilians open the nest after the young hatch and carry the young to the water in their mouths!

A dispute among herpetologists is whether female alligators show parental care by actually guarding the nest. All agree that the female often remains in the vicinity of the nest and in some instances will charge overland toward a person or a predator who approaches too closely. Some accounts maintain that if you stand your ground the female usually will retreat, though few people are willing to play such odds. But suppose you are charged by an adult alligator on land—how fast can it run? Not fast enough or far enough to catch a scared human, adult or child. Reports of alligators running thirty to forty miles per hour on land are pure fantasy.

Alligators simply are not the speed sprinters that some people seem to think.

Some observations about the relationships of alligators to other animals have not yet been formally recorded in the scientific literature, although the phenomena have been noted by laymen and ecologists who work around them. For example, most turtles that live in habitats frequented by alligators are large. Turtles are indeed a major food item of alligators, hence the smaller ones soon become meals. Only the big ones have a fighting chance, and even they have to be careful. Water snakes and cottonmouth moccasins, likewise, are often uncommon in the aquatic areas with alligator populations, presumably for the same reason. A poisonous cottonmouth is no threat at all to the heavily armored alligator.

Alligators are an environmental benefit in some natural systems. For example, many successful heron and egret rookeries in the South are on small islands whose surrounding waters are patrolled by alligators. The discouragement to predators, such as raccoons and opossums, that would have to swim to the island to raid the nests of eggs or young is apparently a significant factor in the ecology of the birds. Few animals can safely enter waters where alligators live.

Another feature of alligator ecology that inadvertently becomes a blessing to certain creatures results from their digging "gator holes." A gator hole is a deep excavation under the bank or into the bottom of a shallow water area. The holes serve as protective retreats for both young and adults. In most instances, the gator hole is the last place that contains water in a lake or swamp that is drying up. A recent scientific study, conducted during a major drought in the Big Cypress Swamp in Florida, showed gator holes to be the last refuge of numerous species of fish. Also, they were presumably the last water holes left for thirsty birds and mammals. Paradoxically, the alligator becomes a benefactor to the very animals on which it depends for food.

As with most potentially dangerous animals that have been poorly studied, the legends and lies are rampant. Alligators have awesome, yet for the most part undeserved, reputations for violence. This myth is probably a holdover from the reports of early settlers that suggest that American alligators once were more bold and assertive than is true today. In addition, the rare but spectacular reports of what appear to be unprovoked attacks on humans keep alive an awareness that alligators can be highly dangerous. Also, the true tales about Old World crocodiles have not helped public opinion about American alligators.

One unusual characteristic that alligators may share with another group of reptiles, the turtles, is their longevity. Turtles and crocodilians of all types are noted for living long periods in comparison to our standards for most other animals. But when the facts are sought the results are somewhat disappointing. Although alligators are sometimes thought of as living indefinitely, few authentic records of American alligators kept in captivity for more than thirty or forty years have been reported. So, although alligators may be able to live more than a century, little or no evidence exists to state this possibility as a fact.

What is the alligator's future? The strict laws against poaching have saved the alligator and have allowed it to regain its population numbers, which are often enormous in some parts of Florida and Louisiana. But federal and state laws already are beginning to relax. In some coastal areas the alligator is now recognized as threatened but not endangered. Legally, threatened species enjoy some level of protection from molestation, but state wildlife officials have greater authority over their control and manipulation than they do for endangered species. In some parts of Louisiana a controlled hunting season now is permitted.

As many environmentalists see the alligator issue, we humans, once again, simply will not sit back and let Nature take her course. Some maintain that for centuries alligators were the dominant biological force shaping natural aquatic environments of the South. They say we should allow these ecosystems to return to normal.

On the other side of the issue are the facts of the increase in numbers of alligators, their encroachment on some suburban areas, and the slight but ever-possible danger to humans and their pets. In contrast to some of the African and Asian crocodiles, wanton attacks by alligators on humans rarely are reported. However, extensive verification exists that they will eat small dogs.

The formidable appearance of alligators belies their natural shyness toward humans. According to hospital authorities in Miami and Houston, fewer than a dozen injuries from American alligators

Ecologists prepare to measure a twelve-foot American alligator in South Carolina. The unusually large specimen came from the federally protected lands of the Savannah River Plant. The protected reservoir inadvertently became a sanctuary for alligators during periods of heavy poaching throughout the United States in the 1950s and 1960s.

are reported each year, whereas each area has more than five thousand recorded dog-bite victims! In fact, the State of Florida Game and Fish Commission has recorded an average of fewer than five alligator bites per year in the last decade. For a region with 9 million permanent residents and more than 32 million visitors per year, the incidence of alligator bites can be considered negligible. Alligators have a long way to go before being considered a serious threat to people in the South.

The clash between attitudes of whether humans should completely dominate the world's environments and all of its plants and animals will not be settled in time to spare the American alligator from untold losses. Alligators are easy to kill, and if they again become marketable they won't have a chance. Once their slaughter

How to Catch an Alligator • 69

is permitted anywhere, illegal poaching will occur in nonlicensed areas. But one important law, if upheld on a worldwide basis, can continue to protect the species forever in areas where human safety is not at stake. That law bans the sale of hides of the American alligator or any crocodilian. If commercialization can be prevented, the American alligator probably will survive as long as the rest of us and remain a natural part of our southern heritage.

Ecologists and everybody else have a world of opinions and attitudes about the world's crocodilians, particularly the American alligator, because of the facts, limited though they are, that have come to light. The knowledge necessary to permit people to have opinions has been collected over many years by many ecologists dealing in raw data. However, when the answers are not clear, ecologists, like other scientists, tend to speculate. This procedure is of course necessary when one studies a form of life that is extinct, such as certain of the large dinosaurs in a group called the Archosaurians, whose only living members are the crocodilians. In an exercise in paleoecological speculation, for example, in what kind of environment did a fifty-ton *Brontosaurus* live? Because the most obvious feature of dinosaurs such as these was their large size, the assumption always has been that their major habitat had to be aquatic. Presumably, in holding up such a massive frame, the buoyancy of water was required. But we don't really know. Maybe they just plodded across prairie scenes like extra-large elephants and used their long necks to reach the tops of tall trees.

Another idea about the ecology of dinosaurs is that some of the smaller ones hunted in packs. The evidence based on fossil records and the hunting habits of present-day animals has been circumstantial. For example, species that hunt alone, such as foxes or bobcats, seldom attack an animal larger than themselves. However, pack hunters, such as wolves or lions, often will take on prey much bigger than any single member of the pack. Some of the large, plant-eating dinosaurs are thought to have been major food items for the smaller, flesh-eating species. Speculation has proceeded that perhaps these smaller dinosaurs demonstrated pack-hunting behavior. Until very recently no evidence had been presented that any modern-day reptile species actually hunts in packs. However, young iguanas now have been observed leaving

Stegosaurus, an enormous, plant-eating reptile, was found in the United States about 60 million years ago. The function of the plates along the back and sides is unknown, but they may have been a form of protection or a means of heating and cooling. (Drawing by Jean Baldwin Coleman)

their nest area and traveling through their environment as a tiny but voracious pack of insect-eating lizards.

The enormous reptile *Stegosaurus* represents another example of speculative paleoecology. The function of the huge row of bony plates down the back of these Jurassic giants has been a mystery to paleontologists from their first discovery. Although the actual function of these projections along the spine and tail is still unknown, most textbooks speculated that they served as a protective armor against such predators as *Tyrannosaurus rex* with its six-inch-long teeth. However, a recent report suggests that the large plates along the back of *Stegosaurus* served as temperature-regulating devices. Evidence based on physics and mathematics indicates that the plates were used as natural solar heating panels. The animal's body was heated and cooled by turning the plates toward or away from the sun. Otherwise, how could such a large animal maintain its body temperature? The time required to increase its body temperature by basking in the sun would leave little time for other activities. Besides, imagine how hot the surface of the skin would become before the insides of such a massive beast were warmed only a few degrees.

Why spend time understanding what reptiles and amphibians used to do? The answer is straightforward. Formulating questions and trying to understand the biological past allows us to look at the biological present more intensively and with different perspectives. A knowledge of the past may give us unexpected insight into environmental phenomena of the present—for today we are caught in a paradox. We know a lot about the lives and environments of certain plants and animals and can impressively demonstrate such knowledge. Yet we are only skimming along the surface in most instances. The public is impressed by television presentations that can make the surface look fascinating without really going beneath it. Scientists are impressed by other scientists who dip below that surface and make a contribution about why the surface looks the way it does. Thus, our scientific knowledge of alligators is primarily superficial whereas we know far more about the private lives of less-celebrated organisms. Indeed, we know a lot of facts in the general fields of ecology and herpetology. But it is far too early to develop a complacency that we know anywhere near enough or that we yet have the wisdom to put these facts to their best use.

CHAPTER 5

The Lizards:

When Blowguns and Nooses Have Unusual Uses

I was on my back, using my elbows to move feet-first down the sloping sand floor. I was fourth in the six-man line of back crawlers. My headlamp was of little use, for when I stared directly upward the ceiling was fewer than six inches above my forehead. The passage was perhaps three feet in width. Narrow. Very narrow. Any normal person would have felt claustrophobic, and I felt very normal. As a herpetologist, I had no business lying on the sandy incline of a tunnel several hundred feet inside a west Texas gypsum cave. But somehow Don Tinkle, who at that time was on the faculty of Texas Tech University, had convinced me to help him with a study that could be conducted only in this manner.

"Listen," he said from the front of the line. To be sure, we did. We all stopped. I tilted my head forward to direct the light beam between my feet and over the top of three outstretched bodies further down the incline.

A chill traveled up the line of bodies with the speed of spoken sound. "Listen" is the last word you want to hear in a gypsum cave. Gypsum is a stratified rock with structural properties that allow layers to slide upon one another. I had been told that if you're in a cave that begins to slip, you could be closed off from the outside world forever. I listened for the grinding.

I was hoping to hear the high buzz of a western diamondback like the one we had caught coiled in the cave's entrance. I hoped it was just another rattlesnake, one that had crawled deep into the cool cave to escape the Texas sun. Any of us could handle a rattlesnake—but not sliding gypsum.

After a few moments I tuned into a far different sound, something you would expect from a dozen little boys trying to sound like chugging locomotives—a combination of puffing and whooshing.

Someone murmured, "Bats," and I saw my first one of the day. It came up the tunnel with more finesse than I have ever seen in an animal. Slipping between a pair of boots, skimming over the brim of a hat, and then gliding with a gentle undulation alongside me. The bat looked into my light with tiny black eyes as it brushed by with a whispery sound.

I turned my light back down the incline where the sound of a loud wind seemed to be approaching. Another lone bat fluttered up the tunnel, faster than the first one. All of our lights were fixed on the bottom of the tunnel as the roaring grew louder. Someone below me shouted as furry brown creatures began to fill the cave tunnel from the bottom. I hurriedly zipped my windbreaker up to my neck and crossed my hands over my chest. I craned forward so my light would show me the length of the tunnel.

The first dozen or so whizzed over my face or beside my head. But as the numbers thickened, they began to collide with the sand, with the walls, and with us. One landed in the center of my windbreaker and began walking up in an awkward, stumbling fashion. Before it reached its takeoff point on my headlamp, it had climbed onto my chin and scrambled across my face. Five or six more landed on my dungarees or jacket and began their ascent toward the top of the tunnel. Unfortunately my face lay between them and their destination. And for no less than ten minutes hundreds of Mexican free-tail bats used my lower torso as a landing strip and my forehead as a launching pad. Only one got misdirected enough to begin walking up the inside of my pants leg. Despite the cramped quarters, my other foot swiftly and firmly pushed it out. I kept my ankles crossed from that point. The army of walking wings finally subsided to a few individuals that were able to maintain their flight up the tunnel without landing.

We finally continued down the tunnel to a larger passageway at the bottom where we could stand and exchange impressions. By comparison, the rest of the day was as uneventful as home gardening. We put leg bands on a few hundred baby bats that were clinging to the ceiling in the nursery chamber and got back out of the cave without seeing another adult bat. When we reached the cave's entrance, there was still enough light to see, and I relaxed.

We climbed to the canyon rim and somewhere to the west I saw half a dozen silhouettes flitting above the tops of the stand of cottonwood trees. They were out a little earlier than bats normally are, and I felt a peaceful communion with them, knowing that two hours earlier we had had a rather close association.

Most of my experiences with animals other than reptiles or amphibians have emanated from a herpetological endeavor that has taken a twist, such as the cave situation, a consequence of an involvement with lizards. Lizards in the Chihuahuan desert of western Texas had been the topic of attention for that entire summer up to the point when we went to the bat cave. To Don Tinkle, taking a day off to look at bats was an appropriate diversion for biology students like ourselves. After all, we spent every day from just after dawn until darkness walking through prescribed sections of the desert in a never-ending search for side-blotched lizards as part of Tinkle's monumental study of the species. Getting away from the sun by going into a cave for a few hours seemed reasonable to all of us.

Most herpetologists begin their careers as snake collectors, often at a very young age, and at first they know little about the other groups of reptiles and amphibians, except as potential food sources for pet snakes. Lizards were never particularly abundant in the Southeast, where I initiated my childhood career as a snake collector, so I knew less about lizards than I did about turtles or frogs or salamanders. But in the Southwest one has ample opportunity to experience a diversity of lizard fauna unparalleled in the rest of the United States.

Lizards represent the largest extant group of reptiles, the more than 3,300 species constituting 57 percent of the known reptilian species in the world. Herpetologists recognize eighteen family groups, eight of which occur in the continental United States. Lizards are worldwide in distribution, excluding Antarctica, and one species is even found above the Arctic Circle. A majority of the species occur in the tropics and more than half belong to the families of skinks and geckos.

As a rule lizards are most common in warm regions of the world, particularly in the wet tropics but also in arid regions. Australia, the driest of the continents, has more than three hundred species of lizards. The numbers of species in the South American tropics is higher, however, and new species are discovered each year. The United States has only about seventy species of lizards, of which only fifteen are native east of the Mississippi. The remainder, with few exceptions, live in the arid Southwest. Arizona alone is the home of forty-four species of lizards.

Lizards and snakes are closely related in a scientific sense and are placed in the same taxonomic order. In fact, using the man-made taxonomic designations, snakes and lizards are more closely related (by being in the same order) than bobwhite quail and mourning doves or rabbits and rats. Few characteristics categorically distinguish these two groups of reptiles. Although snakes never have well-developed legs, a few species have vestigial hind limbs. Some lizards lack limbs, although most have four and a few have only two. But most lizards without legs have eyelids whereas snakes never do. Also, legless lizards usually have ear openings on the side of the head, whereas snakes lack true ear bones and have no opening for sound to enter. Other differences between snakes and lizards involve bone and tooth structure and are not readily discernible to a nonherpetologist.

I had never tried very hard to catch or observe lizards, let alone try to learn much about them, before my experience in Texas. In the Chihuahuan desert you soon find out that if you are to learn much of anything about daytime animals, lizards are one of the better choices. In fact, that was one reason Don Tinkle had picked the group to work with, because in the desert, with the exception of lizards, most terrestrial vertebrates come out at night.

Among the fascinating behavioral features of lizards are the various means of locomotion, the diversity of which is rivaled by no other group of reptiles or amphibians. Most species use the traditional approach of running on four legs. However, some, such as the large leopard lizards and collared lizards of the Southwest, do their fastest running on their two rear legs, bringing forth some ancient memory of what some of the dinosaurs must have looked like. One group, the basilisks of Central and South America are so effective in this two-legged running style that they will actually pad rapidly across small bodies of water without a break in their stride.

As mentioned above, some lizards, like snakes, have no legs. The glass lizards (also called glass snakes) of America and the slowworms of Europe are lizards that rely on undulating movements to propel themselves across a surface or even through sand. One of the most bizarre forms of locomotion by a lizard is observed in the so-called flying dragon of Borneo. Although a four-footed creature that normally climbs on trees, a flying dragon on occasion will leap from a tall tree, spread between the front and hind legs a lateral membrane that is supported by several thin movable ribs, and glide to another tree in the manner of a flying squirrel. The flying gecko of Asia also performs aerially, using not only a lateral membrane but also webbing between the toes and flaps along the tail. Another unusual form of locomotion not yet even reported in the scientific literature is that of the *Polychrus* lizards of Brazil. In this species the male mates with the female and then climbs on her back and rides around wherever she goes for the next day, warding off any other would-be suitors.

Another day-to-day behavioral aspect of lizards involves how they protect themselves from the many predators that would try to make them a meal. Among the chief predators of lizards are birds, snakes, and certain other lizards. Leopard lizards, for example, depend on smaller species of lizards for a major portion of their diet. Among the forms of predator avoidance by lizards are camouflage, speed, and secretiveness. An interesting defensive behavior of certain basilisk lizards of the American tropics is the use of their long tails in whiplike fashion to lash out at any threat, including a human. Lizard tails are perhaps the most widespread means of escaping predators through a form of trickery. Try to catch a fence lizard or a little brown skink and you might end up with a wiggling tail and no lizard. The tails of some species can be broken off by the lizard itself before it is even touched. Then, while the broken tail twists and turns on the ground, the rest of the lizard hastily retreats to cover. Although the tail may be lost to save the individual's life, the loss is only temporary. The regeneration of the tail is characteristic, although the new tail is usually shorter—but still breakable.

Being venomous is, of course, a means of protection, but, in contrast to the many poisonous species of snakes that occur in the world, only one group of modern-day lizards has used this approach successfully. The only poisonous lizards are the Gila monster of the southwestern United States and the beaded lizard of Mexico. The venom is potentially lethal to a human. However, the lizards are much less effective at administering poison than are the poisonous snakes. The venom glands are located in the bottom jaw, in contrast to snakes in which they are located at the back of the head, nor are the fangs hollow hypodermic needles like those of a snake. Instead the fangs have a center groove along which the venom runs when it is released into the mouth.

Although only two poisonous representatives occur, both have impressive reputations. Gila monsters are notorious for being tenacious biters that are almost impossible to pry loose once they latch on to a finger or foot. This tendency to hold on is one mechanism to assure that the poison eventually will reach the bloodstream of the victim. Fortunately, Gila monster bites are rare, and deaths are even rarer. In fact, this species, now officially declared by the federal government as legally threatened, is in far more danger from us than we are from it.

Among the reptiles, lizards hold few records for size or shape. The smallest lizards in the world belong to the skink and gecko families. Although probably not the smallest, the little brown skink of the southeastern United States attains a length of three inches and weighs less than a nickel, about the size of some of the tiny tropical worm snakes. The largest lizard in the world is the Komodo dragon, an impressive creature discovered in the 1800s on islands in the Indonesian region. Komodo dragons reach sizes of more than ten feet, much smaller than certain of the crocodilians. They are completely terrestrial, stalking live prey in the manner of some of the predatory dinosaurs but also eating carrion when it is available. The Komodo dragon belongs to a family of lizards known as the monitors. Monitors are found throughout the Old World tropics and in deserts, including Australia.

Although subtle differences occur in the shape of lizards, the variations are not great. Some forms are legless but most have four well-developed legs, which are used for rapid movement when the occasion arises. A few species have only a pair of front legs and no rear ones. Certain species have flattened bodies, one of the most dramatic being that of the South American flat-bellied lizard, which escapes predators by slipping into a rock crevice and quickly inflating its body so that it cannot be dislodged.

Although the general shape varies within respectable limits, ornamentation and color pattern among the lizards can be spectacular. Perhaps the most eye-catching are the true chamaeleons of Africa. The males of some chamaeleon species have long hornlike extensions on the head that actually are used in combat with other males during the mating period. (Incidentally, most herpetology books use "chamaeleon" for the African species and "chameleon" for the American species. The difference stems from the fact that the African species belong to the family Chamaeleonidae, whereas species of "chameleons" in other families assume the traditional spelling.) The spiny armor of the American horned toads (also called horned lizards) and the Australian thorny devil likewise give an appearance of someone's science fiction creation. Although harmless to humans, the spines undoubtedly serve as an effective deterrent to certain would-be predators.

The role of color is better known for lizards than for any other group of reptiles. Although certain of the snakes have brilliant reds and yellows, the exact function of these colors is unknown in contrast to the brilliant displays used during courtship by male lizards of some species. The common anole of the Americas uses an enlarged throat sac known as a dewlap, which can be bright red or orange. During territorial displays the dewlap warns other lizards or even large animals to back off. The fence lizards of the southern United States are gray or brown in appearance when seen from above, but during courtship periods the males develop brilliant blue patches on their necks and bellies. The bright color is used in displays against other males during courtship for particular females or for a prime territory. Blue, incidentally, is a color that is seen commonly among lizards but few other reptiles or amphibians in the world.

Besides the use of color for mating purposes, lizards are very similar to birds in that the males usually do all of the displaying, but certain lizards possess a trait that is found in a few amphibians and fishes but in no birds, mammals, or other reptiles. That is, an individual is able to change color in response to its immediate surroundings. The colors range from light green to dark brown. Color change of this nature is functionally of two types. One kind is used by the true chamaeleons of Africa, which sometimes change to the color of the background foliage or tree bark. In other words, when the lizard is on a brown piece of wood it may become brown, whereas if it moves to a large, live leaf, it may turn green. One of the most impressive displays of this trait is that an individual can have one-half of its body totally brown, whereas the other half will be solidly green.

Blowguns and Nooses Have Unusual Uses ● 79

Another type of color change is best represented by the American anole (sometimes also called chameleon), in which color is not dependent on the background but is related to other environmental conditions, such as temperature and moisture. An anole sitting on a palmetto plant during a bright, warm day may indeed appear emerald green, whereas one uncovered among dead leaves in the wintertime will be chocolate brown. Both appear to mimic their surroundings but are in fact responding to temperature, not color. The factors governing color change in lizards are extremely complex and not thoroughly understood, so the phenomenon should in no way be regarded as simplistic.

Lizards are far more versatile in their food habits than their close relatives the snakes, which ordinarily will eat only live animals. To be sure, most lizards are dependent upon live prey for subsistence, but a few species are strict vegetarians and some will eat seeds. Even those that do keep a vegetarian diet, such as the desert iguana, as juveniles eat insects. A few species are true specialists. For example, the marine iguanas of the Galápagos Islands actually will enter the salt water to get marine plants, which they eat underwater or upon returning to the rocky shoreline. The horned lizards of the western United States feed almost exclusively on ants.

One of the major challenges for herpetologists who work with lizards is capturing them. Many of the species are extremely fast, even outrunning a man for short distances. Other species are adept climbers that easily can evade the pursuits of even the best tree-climbing boy in the neighborhood. Still others are difficult to capture because of their inconspicuousness, a result of subterranean lifestyles or cryptic coloration, or simply because they are rare in most areas. However, as with other groups of animals, once their personality is understood, each species has its Achilles heel and can be captured in some manner.

For the fleet-of-foot forms, such as the six-lined racerunner of the Southeast and the numerous related species known as whiptails of the Southwest, only one approach has proved effective. That is, they must be stopped by something that moves faster than they do. Dust shot from a .22 rifle has been used in instances when the lizard's fate was unimportant, such as when they were needed for museum specimens and their death would be inconsequential (to

The most effective technique developed for the live capture of fast-moving lizards has been the blowgun. Projectiles such as corks or ripe olives assure that the lizard is only stunned and not killed. The use of needles or nails in the cork turns the blowgun into a lethal weapon. A blowgun expert can hit a three-inch lizard from forty feet away almost every time.

the collector); but a later development, the blowgun, has permitted such animals to be captured alive in a manner as effective as dust shot. The technique is an old one, based on the dart guns of African pygmies. The lizard blowgun is a simple construction of a four-foot aluminum conduit with corks used as the projectiles. The accuracy that can be achieved for short distances of thirty to forty feet is surprising and results in stopping a fast-moving lizard in its tracks. The cork merely stuns the animal, which can then be picked up; it is seldom seriously injured. A later innovation has been the use of ripe olives instead of corks.

Another lizard-catching technique, developed out West as one might suspect, is noosing. Many lizards can be approached to within a few feet but are intolerant of anyone's trying to get closer. Yet they do not seem to mind if you wave a bamboo pole over their heads, even if a string with a tiny lasso in it is dangling from the

The lizard noose has been used to capture thousands of lizards in reptile studies. Many lizard species will allow an investigator to approach within a few feet and will remain stationary while nooses are slipped over their heads and yanked. The technique does not injure the animals at all so that specimens can be obtained alive.

end. With a little maneuvering you can have a lizard wiggling unharmed in the noose within a few seconds.

Not surprisingly, any animal that is close kin to a snake can be expected to have some measure of superstitious beliefs associated with it. Indeed, lizards are frequently thought to be poisonous even in regions of the country or the world thousands of miles from the two venomous species. The harmless blue-tailed skinks, sometimes called "scorpions," of the eastern United States are dreaded by many. In fact, a major portion of the populace in most regions of the world where lizards abound consider them to be capable of some level of poisonous bite or sting. Many lizards will bite if picked up, but in most instances the result is hardly mentionable.

Another superstition that still has not been laid to rest in the South is the belief that a glass snake (actually a legless lizard) will shatter into pieces if hit and then later piece itself back together. To be sure, the tale has some basis in that a glass snake is more than half tail, an extension that will break free as with other lizards. It is not inconceivable that a couple of powerful licks with a hoe handle would shatter the long tail into two or three writhing pieces plus a body that slithers away. It is not difficult to project what the imagination of a frightened person might do with such an event.

No book on modern reptiles would be complete without mention of the tuatara of New Zealand, a creature believed to be a lizard until 1856. In that year a British scientist announced to the world that the bizarre "lizard," known as *Sphenodon* since its discovery in 1831, only superficially resembled a lizard. Instead it belonged to an ancient and thought-to-be extinct order of reptiles as distinct from lizards and snakes as the turtles and crocodilians are.

Among its aberrant features is a tolerance for cold temperatures that are totally unappreciated by other reptiles. Also, the tuatara has three eyes, although the one in the center of the head, like that found in some lizards, does not see visual images. What the fate of this living fossil will be is uncertain, although present New Zealand laws strictly protect the few remaining colonies. Ironically, current legislation is so protective that even certain forms of research on the species are prohibited because it is believed they would be disruptive to the animals. Perhaps this situation is only one more commentary on the new stage of ecological dilemma we have reached in which the legal constraints necessary to protect a vanishing species keep us from understanding it before it is gone forever.

CHAPTER 6

The Salamanders:

Ohio State 7, Alabama 3, Salamanders 0

Imagine our excitement. Very green graduate students, whipped into a froth about being participants in the capture of an animal of which only one specimen had ever been found. And with not just a species were we concerned, but instead with an entire genus. The generic name was *Phaeognathus*. *Phaeognathus hubrichti* it was called, after the entomologist Leslie Hubricht, who had brought the sole specimen known to science back to the U.S. National Museum in 1960. The specimen had been found under the leaves in a wooded ravine in Butler County, Alabama, by a field team looking for spiders. No other specimen of the genus had been discovered despite countless efforts by herpetologists for nearly two years. Some herpetologists began to question the validity of the specimen. Perhaps it was only a freak individual of a more common species of the many related types of salamanders in the region. But examination and scrutiny by the experts, including Dr. Richard Highton who officially described it, left no question that Hubricht inadvertently had picked up a specimen of what was the first new genus of vertebrates to be described in the United States in my lifetime.

Dr. Ronald Brandon of The University of Alabama was the frothmaker for us. What a shame, he allowed, that here we sat in the spring of 1963, the closest major university (we did not count Auburn) to the "type locality" of the newly described lungless salamander, and we were not searching for more specimens. The type locality of any species of animal in the world, by agreement of the International Zoological Commission, is the place from which the original specimen came. The type locality of *Phaeognathus hubrichti* was near McKenzie, Alabama, less than one hundred miles from Tuscaloosa. I wondered at the time why Dr. Brandon had never before mentioned our lack of interest. I was soon to find out, because within three hours from the initiation of our field trip from the Crimson Tide campus, I met our competition.

We encountered the five herpetologists from Ohio State University about dusk in the local cafe near McKenzie Creek. They were in the other booth when we sat down. Dr. Brandon exchanged greetings with their leader, Dr. Barry Valentine. The rest of us on each side tried to look smug and disinterested while making certain our jacket collars were cocked at the right angle. We finally met them, and guess what? They had come all the way from Ohio that day to look for the second specimen of *Phaeognathus*, just like us! Their expedition seemed to be a territorial offensive in the field of herpetology. We all watched Brandon and Valentine to see what their subtle actions and comments might reveal.

We knew that Valentine and the Buckeyes had us when they "had to run," leaving half-cups of pretty good coffee, two doughnuts, half a ham sandwich, and a piece of apple pie that the waitress brought to the table after the Ohioans had checked out through the cashier. We hadn't even ordered yet, and the game rules didn't permit us to leave until we had ordered and eaten something. Or, at least until Valentine and crew were out of sight.

If the Red Dog Cafe hadn't been closed at 2 A.M. when we finally returned to it, I don't think missing supper would have been so bad. A couple of us did manage a cup of coffee to go before we departed, and we shared the two uneaten doughnuts and apple pie left by Ohio State. But the excitement of a herpetological quest was really all we needed at that point. We roared out onto Highway 31, watching the tail lights of Valentine's Ohio State van blink over the last hill to the south. Night presumably would be the time to catch *Phaeognathus* and each team knew where the other was headed.

After passing their van parked on the road shoulder alongside the bridge over McKenzie Creek, we stopped a hundred feet up the hill. How Brandon knew we would need shovels that night I do not know. But indeed, we would need them. Everybody grabbed his own flashlight and collecting bag and we were off.

The flashlights of Valentine's crew were flitting about along the stream bank in the woods upstream from the bridge. As we started to go downstream, we heard the shout. It sounded like a cheer and we all knew, as we stood in the middle of Highway 31, that none of our team would catch the second red-hills salamander, as the species later came to be called. When we heard a second chorus of shouts and someone yelled something about "another one," we turned to go upstream and join the victors.

They had them, all right. By the time we arrived they had caught three of the mystery salamanders. They let us hold one of the specimens, observe its dark brown to purple coloration, feel its slippery skin, and watch it wiggle and squirm across our hands. They were generous with their catch and with the competitive pressure off they showed us how they did it. Steve Tilley showed me my first one.

We sloshed upstream, illuminating the steep, red clay banks with our flurry of light beams. I saw a tiny head as it ducked back into a hole in the side of the cliff. The salamander's move was quick, but Tilley's shovel was quicker. He carved off a shovel-sized chunk of stream bank and out of the falling clay came the first red-hills salamander I was to catch. A pride came over our crew as we identified ourselves as among the first people to prove that *Phaeognathus hubrichti* really was not a freak.

During the collecting frenzy we tried other techniques, too, such as turning over rocks in the stream, ripping logs asunder, and using a dip net in the deeper pools. We even rubbled one long section of stream bank in trying to find unseen specimens suspected of hiding behind the red clay wall. We had managed to find two in this manner earlier and thus were encouraged to continue searching in such fashion. The McKenzie Creek walls fell like Jericho under our relentless attack.

We caught ten red-hills salamanders that night (the actual score was Buckeyes 7, Crimson Tide 3), sacking them away for the return to respective campuses and museums. Brandon and Valentine published extensively on the basis of specimens collected that night and on more specimens that were to come from future collecting trips. Other herpetologists soon heard of the collecting technique, and they sought the heretofore rare salamander for their own universities' museum collections. Extensive use of the technique over the following months became in essence an attack on the McKenzie Creek stream habitat even to the point that Dr. Robert Mount of Auburn University demanded that the environmental assault be stopped or at least moderated. None of us that night or those to follow knew what the impact of removal of salamanders or the consequences of the diggings might be.

At this time the red-hills salamander is doing as well as can be expected under the environmental circumstances of Alabama and the United States. The species has been found in a few habitats other than McKenzie Creek, but all are nearby in the same region. Fortunately, not every herpetologist within two thousand miles packed up a group of students in a university van and moved into the McKenzie Creek area the same night we did. If this influx had occurred, several hundred yards of a peaceful, southern Alabama creek bank and the red-hills salamander could have suffered appreciably. In reality, even during several years of salamander collecting by herpetologists on McKenzie Creek, the damage to the stream environment really has not been that severe. It has been nothing, actually, in comparison to, say, the construction of a shopping center. So the stream itself is temporarily saved from destruction, by herpetologists or others. But what about salamanders as a group? How are they faring in a modern world?

As a group, salamanders make up a minor portion of the world's animal life. Fewer than four hundred species are known, most are small (few reach a length of six inches), and few are routinely eaten, hunted, or used commercially. Salamanders are one of the largest groups of animals in the world to which North America can lay claim to having a greater number and diversity of species than any other continent.

Herpetologists recognize eight taxonomic or family groupings of salamanders. Representatives of seven occur in the United States, and the members of three families actually are restricted to North America. Salamanders are entirely absent from Australia and only a few species are found in Africa. South America is represented by members of only one of the eight families. The area of greatest salamander density in the world is in the Appalachian Mountains of North Carolina. For example, in one county in western North Carolina, almost thirty species of salamanders, 10 percent of those found in the world, possibly could be found on a single rainy night.

Most salamanders are superficially similar to lizards in having four legs and a long tail, but the resemblance ends there. Where lizards thrive in tropical or warm, arid regions, most salamanders are totally dependent on moist, and in many cases totally aquatic, environments in the temperate zones. Lizards have a dry, scaly skin, whereas salamanders have a moist, slimy skin, which is used to supplement their breathing. In fact, members of one family (the woodland salamanders) are lungless and breathe entirely through their skin. Lizards give birth to their young or, in most species, lay leathery or hard-shelled eggs somewhere on land, whereas most salamanders lay gelatinous-covered eggs in the water or in extremely moist places, such as under moss or rotting logs. No salamanders have claws; they are not poisonous, and, in fact, only a few species can bite hard enough to get your attention.

Among the few kinds that can bite a human hard enough to matter are the congo eels, which reach lengths greater than three feet. They closely resemble but are unrelated to true eels, which are fish. The obvious differences between congo eels and true eels are that the salamanders have two pair of minute legs and no external gills. Another difference is that congo eels have a powerful and effective bite if handled—a point of which the fisherman who lands one should be aware. Once these giant slimy salamanders clamp down and begin their violent twisting, whatever they have taken hold of is probably going to leave with them. The congo eel is restricted to coastal plain habitats from Virginia to Louisiana, a geographic range that is more confined than that of any other family of North American salamanders.

Another family of large eel-like salamanders includes the sirens, which are slimy, aquatic creatures found in streams and lakes of the South and up the Mississippi Valley. Permanent external gills, a pair of tiny front legs, and the absence of back legs give them a most unusual appearance. Sirens are basically inoffensive creatures that actually make excellent, though shy, pets. Specimens of one species reach lengths of more than three feet.

The smallest salamanders in the world are tiny, as may be expected. For example, the dwarf salamander of the southeastern United States attains a maximum size approaching that of a kitchen match. The size of the largest salamanders in the world, however, may come as a jolt. One species in Japan reaches a length of nearly six feet and may weigh more than eighty pounds. A close relative, the hellbender of the eastern United States, may attain a length of close to a yard. Most salamanders, however, are three to six inches long with a tail that is approximately half their total length.

The greater siren is one of the three largest salamanders in North America. It is totally aquatic and has a pair of external gills for respiration. Sirens have a single pair of tiny front legs and no rear ones. Sirens are so slimy that herpetologists must use a sock to pick them up.

Although secretive animals, salamanders display a remarkable breadth of color. The marbled salamander of the eastern United States has a shiny black body ringed by silver saddles that can be breathtaking in appearance when contrasted with the dark organic soil or the inside of a rotten log where it might be found. The common semiaquatic salamander known as the red-spotted newt has a land-dwelling juvenile phase (the red eft) whose bright orange or red skin color would catch the eye of anyone who happens to be out with a flashlight on a rainy spring night in many parts of the eastern United States. The banana-peel yellow of the two-lined salamander found along stream margins of the southern United States comes as a surprise to anyone who discovers the hiding places of such creatures beneath rocks or moss. Citing these colorful specimens is not to suggest that many species, such as the eastern mole salamanders, which look like slate-gray link sausages with legs, are nondescript and unexciting in color.

Color may play a significant biological role for these seemingly defenseless animals, which might appear to be no more than an easy meal to many predators. Most people in the United States are aware of coral snake mimics, such as the scarlet snake or scarlet kingsnake. Each species superficially resembles the other so that the "mimics" benefit by not being eaten by predators that think them venomous. But studies by herpetologists in the last two decades have strongly suggested that salamanders also are an example of the mimic phenomenon. The brightly colored red efts of woodland areas in the eastern United States may seldom be seen above ground; but even when they are seemingly available prey, most animals will not eat them. Why? Because red efts taste terrible and are avoided by most creatures that would otherwise try to devour a small salamander. Recent studies by Dr. Edmund Brodie have tested the effectiveness of the bright red warning color of other salamanders that are much more palatable but superficially resemble the red eft. According to Brodie's studies, in which he and his students actually tasted a variety of different types of salamanders, the efts did have a taste that was definitely unsavory to graduate students and presumably would be noxious or even toxic to other animals. Some of the other species did not taste so bad (for a salamander). However, other species of salamanders, such as the brightly colored red salamander that is taxonomically unrelated to the newts, would be spared from would-be predators by virtue of their close resemblance.

Although newts of the eastern United States may taste bad, the related form known as the rough-skinned newt on the West Coast if eaten actually can be deadly to people as well as to other animals. A visiting herpetologist once told me of seeing a pelican die alongside a lake in western Washington. During its last gasp, the pelican's huge beak fell open and a rough-skinned newt crawled out—presumably a commentary on the cause of death. A recent report from Oregon told of a man who died from eating a newt on a bet.

Salamanders have fewer superstitions about them than do many of the reptiles and other amphibians, but the oldest belief about these animals is indeed noteworthy itself. In the Middle Ages in Europe, salamanders were believed to be able to endure fire. Perhaps the superstition arose from the bright reds, oranges, and yellows of European newts that might have looked like they were on fire. Maybe salamanders occasionally crawled out of the Yule log or other burning wood in which they had made a home, giving an impression of emerging from the fire. Whatever the case, the belief has persisted so that even today the word "salamander" is associated with fire: a salamander is a red-hot iron used for lighting gunpowder, and salamander-hair is another name for asbestos.

The concept of the "spring lizard" is one that has persisted in rural areas of the South and the Appalachians since early settlement days. Clear pools or springs were frequently the focal point of human activities in many areas, and associated with such waters are various species of aquatic salamanders. The origin of the story has long been lost, but lore has it that each spring system has a salamander, a "spring lizard," that is responsible for keeping the water clean, healthy, and running. If the salamander is disturbed in some way and leaves the spring area, the entire system purportedly will dry up. The persistence of this myth in some areas probably has been the salvation of many of the mountain stream salamanders.

One of the bizarre phenomena about salamander natural histories that has been discovered in recent years has been the occurrence of cannibalistic species. Among most groups of animals, there are species that will eat other species in the group. For example, a peregrine falcon will eat a duck, a kingsnake will eat a copperhead. But for individuals of a species to kill and have a steady diet of other members of the *same* species is unusual. However, such cannibalism does occur.

The most studied example of cannibalism among the reptiles and amphibians has been that of tiger salamanders of the western United States. Tiger salamanders are one of the wide-ranging forms of salamanders occurring from New York State throughout the East and into Mexico. Despite their commonness their life history has been poorly understood, partly because of the high variability from one region to another. The basic pattern of reproduction in a tiger salamander population is for individuals to move into temporary woodland ponds during heavy spring rains, to deposit eggs, and then for the adults to depart back to a land-dwelling existence until the next year. However, in some areas, particularly in the western United States, certain of the aquatic larvae never leave the aquatic habitat breeding ponds. Instead they retain their gills and other larval features but they reproduce as adults without ever assuming a terrestrial lifestyle. Although larval salamanders that reproduce are not rare, the development of cannibalistic larvae is. And the cause is completely unknown at this time.

The events leading to cannibalism are that certain members of the population begin to develop huge heads and extraordinarily enlarged, grotesque teeth. The teeth obviously are designed for something more than eating their normal diet of aquatic insects. In fact, they turn out to be ideally suited for grabbing a slippery tiger salamander and holding on until the meal is finished. These nightmarish creatures would make anyone pleased to find out that most salamanders are very small.

Aside from their eating their own kind on occasion, salamanders do not show what humans would consider much imagination in their choice of diets. Most forms subsist on insects or other small, ground-dwelling invertebrates. Some of the larger varieties are known to eat crayfish, frogs, small fish, and snakes. Perhaps more remarkable is the eastern dwarf salamander, which has been found to prey heavily upon small, usually inconspicuous invertebrate organisms known as springtails. These little animals are so tiny that we once found a dwarf salamander with more than two hundred springtails in its stomach.

Despite their being few in number and highly restricted in their geographic distribution, salamanders occupy some unusual habitats. The blind salamanders are represented by three distinctive species in the United States—the grotto salamander, the Texas blind salamander, and the Georgia blind salamander. All are ghostly pale in appearance and as adults are confined to underground caverns. Most specimens that have been collected have been found as a consequence of well-drilling operations or other situations in which subterranean waters are exposed to the surface.

Among the rarest and least-studied of the amphibians is a group known as the caecilians. Caecilians live in tropical areas of the Old and New Worlds with a lifestyle in most instances of burrowing beneath the soil and seldom being seen above ground.

Salamanders are intolerant of salt water or even brackish conditions and are seldom present on island or beach habitats. One group of salamanders has become airborne in a sense, becoming well-adapted to the epiphytic habitats in the tropics. Epiphytes, or "air plants," are species that physically live upon other plants but do not obtain nutrients from them. The phenomenon is particularly prevalent in the wet tropics where certain orchids, ferns, and bromeliads make their homes on tree limbs high above the ground. The epiphytes in turn become the home of tropical salamanders, some of which spend their adult lives within the confines of a single plant. The entire existence of such specialists depends on the environmental welfare of a particular plant species.

Frogs and salamanders represent the two major groups of amphibians to most people, a notion caused in part by our Temperate Zone existence. In the tropics lives the third group of amphibians, the caecilians, which are practically unheard of by most people. Few biologists are familiar with caecilians at all and even fewer have ever seen one alive. Yet, more than 160 species are known to occur in tropical areas of the world, with only limited intrusion into the more temperate climates. Caecilians are like no other vertebrates. They resemble earthworms in lacking legs and having a series of ringlike folds around the body. Their eyes are tiny, ineffective organs. Because of the burrowing habits of the terrestrial species (some are aquatic), their confinement to tropical areas, and perhaps the actual rarity of most species, caecilians are the most poorly studied group of amphibians from an ecological standpoint.

Salamanders and caecilians collectively make up fewer than five hundred species on earth today. Some people might ask, What good are they, and why is it worth knowing anything about them? In some instances ecologists can make a case for a particular species by producing scientific evidence that local environmental impacts may occur as a consequence of the species' loss. The importance of salamanders or caecilians to natural ecosystems is unknown but may be significant in some instances, particularly as prey items for other animals. Or an environmentalist may offer that commercial interests will suffer, or that public attitude and sentiment demand that the species be given appropriate attention. Although none of the species is of major importance to commercial enterprises, to sports or recreation, or to solving food problems, some do make interesting pets. And, of course, the importance of a species for unsuspected medical uses can never be second-guessed. The fact that most people in the world have never seen or perhaps even heard of either group of animals certainly should not be held against them.

It is appealing to learn something about these unassuming creatures of the temperate and tropical regions. They provide us with a mystery that not only needs solving but only just now has been discovered. Perhaps that is the criterion that sets humans and animals apart—people press for the dissolution of ignorance at any level, whether or not the "practical" aspect is at issue. If nothing else, such animals as salamanders and caecilians serve as a reminder to us that we have a responsibility to maintain the distinction.

CHAPTER 7

The Frogs and Toads:

Who's Watching the Frogs?

The day was cool, so scattered patches of late morning fog still rose from the places where water stood. Reaching a height about half that of the taller cypresses, the smoky mist was greeted by a gentle breeze from the south and slowly drifted upward and vanished. Rays of sunlight that had found a passage through the black cypress trunks illuminated the lower clouds of mist. Except for the cease- less racket of a far-off pileated woodpecker and the uncertain flight of a chestnut-sided warbler whose shadow was accentuated by the remaining sunlit fog, it was as though a primeval Carboniferous swamp still existed on earth—centuries before the dawn of terres- trial animals. For a while only a few birds and insects created the effect, then the splashing of an otter was added to the other sounds. The creature swam along the edge of a muddy slough that had stopped being a stream long ago and was only a long, snakelike body of brown water that probably dried up in the summer to be refilled by winter rains. The otter emerged onto the slimy bank, shivered a moment, and then disappeared beneath the twisted roots of a huge cypress. No longer the primeval scene of minutes before, that section of the Savannah River swamp became the scene of millennia later, when the slow evolutionary process had had time to develop animals capable of living, breeding, and dying in this environment. The final touch to this process was added by the presence of humans—Becky Sharitz and me.

When we had first set out on our mission and entered the swamp, we had seen a bobcat atop an ancient live oak that was growing on higher ground near the channel. All-too-full from a successful night hunt, the bronze-eyed hunter had been draped over a large limb near the top of the canopy and was either unconcerned or (more likely) unaware of our presence. We watched the silent predator a long time before moving on, for we see few bobcats in a year's time, although they are still abundant in such unsettled parts of the region. Even when we started the outboard and purred along the winding channel beneath the cat's perch camouflaged by Spanish moss, the swamp's top terrestrial carnivore (since cougars are no longer found in South Carolina or Georgia) kept its place and did not move. As the boat approached a fork we took a smaller channel, shut off the motor, and began to paddle the boat along into the swamp darkness.

We drifted silently along the channel, for paddling was easy in the slight current. I began to look and listen for evidence of the creature we sought. A marsh rabbit, larger than the closely related cottontail, bounded away across a swamp ridge. I imagined that its eyes, soft, brown, and frightened, had watched us from the darkness beneath a fallen palmetto leaf along the dry section of the shoreline—eyes full of the warranted caution and fear befitting a prey species within easy reach of a predator. The rabbit's large ears probably had twitched for sound but heard only the swishing in the water as we, new creatures of the swamp, passed within easy pouncing distance. When the human smell came, moments afterwards, the rabbit fled. To the rabbit our smell was one to learn and possibly fear.

The channel widened into a large black pool. A glint of sunlight sliced through a space between two large cypresses and for an instant our boat cast a long, moving shadow down through the water. From the pool's bottom a fish might judge the dark form of a boat on the water's surface to be that of another inhabitant of the pool, one who fed at night and was the unchallenged ruler of that part of the swamp—for alligators are still common in the Savannah River drainage.

We entered the area of tall trees where bald cypress and tupelo gum stand in water deep enough for a small boat. The SRP swamp forests have gone untimbered for a century, so the trees are big enough to form a heavy canopy but are spaced far enough apart to allow a boat to be maneuvered between their wide trunks. To me, this part of the swamp is magnificent, and I felt good about getting there. As I watched Becky survey the lower canopy with a botanist's eye, seeking information on the new spring growth, I knew she felt the same. A mature cypress-gum swamp is as stately as any forest in the world.

Who's Watching the Frogs? • 97

I was still excited from having seen the bobcat and was anticipatory that the sunny day would lure alligators or turtles to their basking sites. More excitement. Even the occasional garfish or bowfin that churned the water in front of our boat gave a moment's thrill. The swamp is full of adventure to those who are on the lookout, though our actual quarry would be considered far less dramatic than bobcats, alligators, or garfish. We had hoped only to locate a likely collecting spot for the species during the daytime and then return at night to find the specimens. I looked up the tall trunks and wondered where the creatures we were after stayed during the daytime or during cold nights. Did anyone know? As we drifted quietly along listening to birds chatter and to the once-in-awhile splashes of unseen fish, a sound touched me. I motioned for Becky to stop paddling and pointed toward the canopy. Her nod and glance upward showed that she heard it too. The eerie whistle was of neither bird nor insect.

The high-pitched notes sounded near and then distant, creating a ventriloquistic effect. The sound was a strange one, befitting the dark depths of a southern swamp. But we were more than pleased with our find. Without even having to return after nightfall we had verified the presence of the bird-voiced tree frog in the SRP swamp.

The species is classified as Of Special Concern on South Carolina's list of environmentally notable species of plants and animals. Since that spring day when we had set out to find likely habitats where bird-voiced tree frogs *might* be, many specimens have been seen, heard, and collected from that part of the river swamp. They still are considered uncommon in most parts of South Carolina and are restricted to areas of cypress-gum swamp where their weird song may dominate an otherwise silent swamp forest at night.

The eastern United States has thirty-five species of frogs and toads, each with its own distinctive shape, size, color, behavior pattern, and characteristic song. The twenty-two species, besides the bird-voiced tree frog, that occur on the SRP are distributed among five families. The ecology of any of the SRP species is poorly understood, as is true of most frogs throughout the world. Ecological blind spots exist even for the bullfrog, the most widespread amphibian species in the United States. For example, do bullfrog tadpoles at cooler latitudes take one or two years to develop into

98 ● *The Frogs and Toads*

The bullfrog, largest North American frog, is native to the eastern United States but now is found in aquatic habitats throughout the country where human beings have transplanted the species. Frogs are carnivorous, and the bullfrog has been known to eat small turtles and snakes, birds, mice, and even baby alligators.

frogs? Biologists are not sure. This simple question is difficult to answer, for field research requires great caution on the part of observers, lest they inadvertently influence the system they are watching—for how do you study a bullfrog tadpole without bringing it into the laboratory where it is impossible to duplicate a natural environment and where you know its behavior will be altered?

The diet of bullfrogs is well known. Numerous dissection studies have shown that bullfrogs will eat any living animal they can get into their enormous mouths. Small snakes, other frogs (including bullfrogs), baby turtles, mice, and of course insects all have been found in bullfrog stomachs. Two scientists from Alabama reported

Who's Watching the Frogs? ● 99

finding a large male bullfrog in the process of eating a full-grown songbird, a species of warbler. My own experience with the feeding habits of bullfrogs includes a unique incident involving one we kept in a terrarium. One day I put a hatchling alligator that was presumably too small to harm the bullfrog into the terrarium. We were right not to worry about the frog. After thirty seconds, the bullfrog had finished off its first meal of the day!

A threatened species of frog, the pine barrens tree frog occurs in South Carolina. Scientists first became aware of the species in 1854 when a specimen was sent to the U.S. National Museum in Washington for identification. The postmark, Anderson, South Carolina, provided the frog's scientific name, *Hyla andersoni*. None of these little green frogs with the grape-colored stripe down the side has been seen in the vicinity of Anderson since then. In fact, in South Carolina the pine barrens tree frog currently is known from only a few acres, and choruses are observed only a few summer nights each year in the Carolina Sandhills National Wildlife Refuge in Chesterfield County. Even in the New Jersey pine barrens, where the greatest concentrations of these frogs are found, the first specimen was caught in 1862 and the second not until 1889.

In 1976 we set about trying to find this elusive species on the SRP because it once was reported from the general region, and we wished to verify the presence of all rare and threatened species on the SRP site. Dr. Julian Harrison of the College of Charleston is an expert on South Carolina amphibians, so we spent a day looking for suitable habitats, as Becky and I had done for the bird-voiced tree frog. We did not expect to find a pine barrens tree frog in the daytime, but at night we returned to the most likely sites.

The seasonal dryness worked against us. Although some frogs routinely call from the water's edge, the pine barrens tree frog seldom has been heard except during thunderstorms. Dr. Harrison came prepared, however, and at each habitat he played a tape recording of a chorus of pine barrens tree frogs. Each time the night stillness was broken by the recording, something responded. Cricket frogs, silent when we arrived at one lake, began their chirping in response to the recording, which also included a small chorus of this species. The hoot of a barred owl could be heard in the background on the recording, and at four places on the SRP barred owls actually answered the tape's call. One even perched in a small pine tree beside us and challenged the recording directly with a series of authoritative hoots only six feet from where Julian and I stood in amazement. Once a single frog in a natural seepage area replied to the quacking sound of the taped frog chorus. But when we finally found and caught it, on the trunk of a bay laurel tree, it turned out to be a green tree frog, a common species.

One site, a freshwater habitat we call Steel Creek Bay, is unusual on the SRP in having a sphagnum moss mat that covers the ground. Carpenter frogs were calling when we arrived that night. Neither sphagnum moss nor carpenter frogs are common on the SRP but both are known associates of the rare pine barrens tree frog. We played the tape again, and across the tree-lined marshy flat we heard a lone reply—a faraway quonking sound that neither of us recognized as any of the common species of tree frogs. Was it a pine barrens tree frog? We are not sure, for we were never able to find the lone caller. To this day, no pine barrens tree frog has been caught on the SRP, but each time we have afternoon and evening thunderstorms during warm weather I have a tingling inside that urges me to go to Steel Creek Bay and see if pine barrens tree frogs are really there.

A herpetologist makes no scientific distinction between frogs and toads, although a bullfrog is obviously a "frog" and a garden toad is obviously a "toad." To some people, toads have warts and frogs do not; toads live in dry habitats whereas frogs are around water; frogs jump long distances, toads hop. But as what does the narrow-mouthed toad (or frog) qualify? It has a squat body but smooth skin. It lives on land most of the time but enters the water to breed and lay eggs. It kind of hops. Clearly the terms are colloquial and are probably best left undefined, to seek their own levels in conventional usage.

Frogs (the general term for frogs or toads) are the most widely distributed of the reptiles and amphibians, occurring north of the Arctic Circle and southward to Tasmania. Some species, such as the cascades frog, are found at elevations above nine thousand feet in the Cascade and Olympic mountains of the American Northwest. A species of frog is the only amphibian that can tolerate salt water. The crab-eating frog of Southeast Asia actually lives in tidal pools, a feat that would be lethal to all other amphibians in the world. Most frogs are restricted to freshwater habitats, although some species, such as the green tree frog, do have a limited tolerance to brackish water systems. Frogs are unevenly distributed geographically. The greatest numbers of species and individuals occur in the tropics of both the New and Old World. Dr. William Duellman of the University of Kansas has described more than thirty new species of tree frogs in Central and South America within the last decade.

The continent (excluding Antarctica) with the lowest number of frog species is Australia, with fewer than 160 species of naturally occurring frogs, representing only four of the two dozen families known to occur in the world. Perhaps the arid nature of much of Australia accounts for the paucity of frogs. Although a few species are adapted for dry conditions, most are found in high moisture areas. The United States has only about fifty species of frogs, the greatest concentrations occurring in the humid Southeast, but the scores of species found in Mexico boost North America's total far above that of Australia's.

Frogs are different from all other groups of vertebrate animals in that the adults have no tails. This fact is something that only an anatomy student might find noteworthy at first; but, when one considers that almost all mammals (with the notable exception of humans), birds, fishes, reptiles, and other amphibians have apparent if not functional tails, one wonders how such a condition might have evolved in an entire group of animals represented by more than two thousand species. One hypothesis is that in the evolution of an animal that hopped great distances (relative to its length) a tail was an encumbrance that natural selection gradually eliminated. What we see today in rabbits and hares with their powder puff tails supports such an explanation. Unfortunately, as is often the case in evolutionary speculation, the kangaroo is an embarrassment to this argument because kangaroos hop but also have tails, although a kangaroo's tail is specially adapted for the way the kangaroo hops. Although Kipling might have been able to explain "how the frog lost its tail," an academic discussion among biologists of why the frog has no tail likely would not have a clear resolution. As Nature always has it, there is an exception—the tailed frog of the American Northwest. The male has a tail that, rather than being used for swimming in the clear mountain streams where the species is found, is used as a mechanism for placing sperm in the female. This species is the only living member of the order of frogs that has been found with any form of tail-like structure, although the fossil ancestors of modern frogs had tails, as do all tadpoles.

Despite the drab olive color of a bullfrog or the nondescript brown of the common garden toad, frogs and toads exhibit a wealth and variety of colors and patterns. One of the most common species in the Southeast is the green tree frog, with its bright emerald body and yellow racing stripe down each side. The western green toad is also attractive, but, rather than being bright and striking in appearance, the color is a powdery, soft, almost pastel green. Although shades of green are the predominant colors of most frogs, certain species of the poison arrow frogs of Central America are a bright red, orange, or vermilion. The golden frog of Central America is a startling yellow.

Frogs cannot compete with any of the reptiles or even with salamanders for large size. But those who think the American bullfrog holds the record may be in for a surprise. To be sure, the bullfrog is the largest of the frogs in North America, the record size approaching a weight of two pounds and a length, outstretched, of close to eighteen inches. However, the giant frog of Africa attains a maximum weight approaching five pounds and when outstretched can be more than two feet in length. Attempts have been made by enterprising frog ranchers to crossbreed this species with the American bullfrog to produce large, high-quality frog legs. The efforts have been unsuccessful. One species of frog does challenge the record for being the smallest among the reptiles and amphibians. The Cuban grass frog attains an adult length of one-fourth inch and weighs less than a dime. The little grass frog of Florida and the coastal states whose chirp sounds no louder than a trapped insect's buzzing is the smallest of the U.S. frogs, the maximum size being slightly over one-half inch.

The males of almost all species of frogs have distinctive calls, such as the deep-throated rumble of a southern bullfrog, the laughter of a leopard frog, the eerie trill of a bird-voiced tree frog, the sheeplike bleating of a narrow-mouthed toad, or a sound like a yard full of baby chicks created by a chorus of oak toads. A male frog calls to attract mates or possibly, in some species, to designate his territory to other males, as is the fashion of some birds. A recent study has discovered that frogs alter and modify their calls to avoid predation from an unexpected source, bats. Certain species of tropical bats actually feed on certain frog species whose calls can be detected by the flying predators, which attack their prey with pinpoint accuracy. As a defense for this unusual form of predation, some frogs alter their call pattern by becoming ventriloquists so that the bats become disoriented, or else they mimic the calls of frog species that have poisonous glands on top of their heads and that are avoided by the bats.

Although we all know that garden toads and frogs along a pond eat countless numbers of noxious insects every day (or night), their primary contribution to natural environmental systems may be as food for certain snakes or other animals and to provide animal noises on rainy nights, when no other creature does. Frogs unquestionably add a spark to Nature's presentation of life. Provided with the proper knowledge, a close look at frogs and toads, as with any group of plants or animals, will reveal something of interest. Instilling this desire to learn and look is the most serious challenge of the ecologist.

CHAPTER 8

Techniques in Herpetology:

To Catch a Cooter

The people and organizations who support ecological research usually do not realize how much time must go into the failures before a successful technique is developed. It seems to be accepted practice in medicine to try everything until we develop the cure and then once the cure is found to decide the efforts were all worthwhile. The same is true in ecological research and it is only fair that scientists report their failures so that others will not try them again. However, reporting a failure is not the style of most people, including myself, and it is only following success, if even then, that one dares talk about the failures that led to it.

We have developed numerous techniques and approaches in the study of herpetology that have been successful. But in some ways certain of the failures were greater adventures than attempts that turned out right. One that comes to mind started on a day in late spring 1979 at the Savannah River Ecology Laboratory. We needed a sample of river cooters. They were important for a turtle study we had in progress. The river cooter was one species of turtle for which we had not been able to obtain samples.

We had taken a number of excursions up and down the Savannah River to see literally hundreds of cooters basking on fallen trees along the river. We had tried trapping them, to no avail, because cooters do not eat fish or other bait as readily as most turtles; instead they eat vegetation. You might ask, why not bait your trap with vegetation? But why should a turtle go into a trap to get vegetation that is all around it anyway? No, something else would have to be tried.

We did find that some individuals could be approached closely with a motor boat, and in fact we were able to catch one or two this way, but that took half a day. Then we tried using a shotgun to shoot them off the logs. The problem with that is that if you are far enough away in a boat for the turtle not to become wary, then you are too far away to grab it in time before it falls off the log after being shot. The brown Savannah claims anything that goes beneath the surface. Shooting turtles off logs from a boat did not work either.

Finally, we arrived at what surely would be the perfect technique: inner tubes. Using inner tubes would allow us to float downriver to a log with turtles while carrying a shotgun or rifle to shoot the specimen from close range so it could be captured a split second after being shot. Garfield Keaton and Ray Semlitsch designed our floats, and we gave it a try.

Frequently in field research you feel you are given a warning and then another warning, and always when you look back you wish you had taken the first one as advice. Sure enough, before we reached the river that day, we received our first warning. The region had received more than two inches of rain the previous day and the level of the river was up almost six feet. The day was beautiful with clear skies, almost cool in the morning, but because water had been released from Clark Hill reservoir that night, the river was definitely up. We had a four-wheel-drive truck as we took the dirt road toward Jackson Landing through the bottomland hardwood forest. Soon we were hubcap deep in water that seemed to be getting gradually deeper. Someone unfamiliar with this southern swampland might have marveled at oak-hickory woods where all the trees were standing in water, but such flooding happens often.

I was driving, trying to stay in the road, which looked more like a stream channel, when Garfield lifted his feet and remarked that they were wet. Next Ray was exclaiming, "Pick the rifles up!" as he scrambled for the guns that we had put behind the back seat on the floor. My error was in opening the door, intending to look down to see how far the water was below us, only to realize that the water level was almost a foot above the floor of the truck. Ray did save the rifles as the brown wave washed into the truck and left us sitting shin deep in Savannah River floodplain water.

We rescued everything we could, such as lunches, extra ammunition, and a plastic bag someone had brought with certain essentials in it. After recovering the items on the floor, we realized that the engine had stopped. Small wonder, because we had entered a hole in the road that put the water level at three feet in the region of the front wheels. Fortunately, or so we thought at the time, we had our inner tubes already outfitted for the trip and, being only a quarter of a mile of wet road from the river, there was nothing else to do but begin the river trip before we had intended to. We carried the rifles and dragged the inner tube floats. We placed the other paraphernalia on the little platforms on the inner tubes. It was a long muddy walk, mostly through water, with a few deep holes but a few high spots with grass and ground. At last we arrived at the banks of the Savannah River, which was wasting no time getting from Augusta to the Atlantic Ocean 180 river miles away.

Being far more clever than turtles, the three of us had designed a mechanism for approaching closely enough to shoot and catch them before they fell into the water. With the inner tube float system to support us and our guns, our only remaining weakness, or so it seemed, was some form of concealment. Obviously, the river current would sweep us down toward the logs where the turtles were basking and it seemed obvious that something a turtle would be least likely disturbed by would be a limb floating in the water. Therefore we proceeded to cover ourselves and our inner tubes with twigs and vines and leafy branches so that each of us would look like a small tree lazily drifting down the flooded river. It was going to be so easy that we were in good spirits by the time we put the first inner tube in the water, even though we still had a pickup truck stranded in three feet of water.

My inner tube went in first, looking like a small vegetated island. I placed my rifle in the center of the platform and stretched my body out. Upon pushing away from shore, I found the current to be swifter even than it looked, and I was whisked away from Ray and Garfield before I knew what was happening. I got to be the first of us to find out that we had little control over where the inner tube went or which way it turned. After the initial sweep toward the center of the river and the state of Georgia the current brought me swiftly back toward the South Carolina side where I was moving along at a fast rate toward an overhanging tree limb. Everything had happened so fast that I was still trying to organize my rifle, my lunch, and the other items that were in the plastic bag and figure some way to get control of this rogue inner tube. My balance was precarious at best and upon hitting the overhanging tree limb the inner tube flipped one direction, I fell another, and the rifle and plastic bag went their way. The most important thing on my mind at the moment was to save that rifle, and I caught it as the barrel went into the water. The inner tube scooted away from me and the plastic bag went floating downstream. Although the inadequacy of the platform design was revealing itself at every moment, Garfield had thought of one feature that worked well. The inner tube did not get away from me as I clutched the overhanging limb trying to keep myself and the rifle out of the water. The reason the inner tube stayed around was that we each had tied ropes around our waists and then to the inner tubes in the unlikely event that someone tipped over, as I had just done. Ten minutes later I finally had recovered the plastic bag from one hundred feet downstream where it was lodged against a fallen log and had situated myself in the water holding on to the inner tube and simply using the platform to carry the rifle and plastic bag. During this time Garfield and Ray had drifted by me, sitting on their platforms. They looked very smug and confident as I anxiously waited for the first overhanging branch one of them should encounter.

We had left around noon and made arrangements to be picked up in two hours at another landing approximately twelve miles away. It seemed reasonable to me that a river moving about six miles an hour ought to carry an inner tube twelve miles in two hours. How I ever managed to miscalculate by four hours I do not know. But even though we began almost on time, the trip in the river took six full hours, yielded not one turtle, and left us cold, sunburned, and totally exhausted by the time we had floated the whole distance.

We learned a lot though. River cooters are wary of inner tubes surrounded by vegetation, and it almost seemed that they were amused as they dove into the water many yards before we ever got to a log where they were basking. Turtles are not supposed to be able to laugh, but now I am not sure. Six hours is a long time to while away with two-thirds of your body in cold river water, so we had plenty of time to look, meditate, fire the shotgun straight up in the air and let the pellets fall down on us, and watch for unusual animals. With modern transportation one seldom has the opportunity to travel along the river without making waves and noise that would frighten away most of the wildlife before you see it. I was indeed impressed at how many more animals were there than we normally saw.

We drifted to a sandbar where a large alligator perhaps ten feet long was basking, a seldom-seen sight in this region. Our technique apparently worked well for animals that do not spend their life worrying about what is sneaking up on them through the water. Pileated woodpeckers made the river corridor sound like jackhammers when we passed through the deep pine areas, and prothonotary warblers skittered around in the shoreline vegetation, their bright yellow heads seemingly out of place in the dark swamp gloom. We also were able to float up alongside many water snakes draped over the shoreline vegetation. But, despite our seeing what a quiet, unmotorized trip down a river can be like, we never were able to approach the ever-wary river cooters that we had set out to catch. They clearly were the winners of the contest that day, because of a technique that did not work.

Techniques may seem a trivial issue in the world of sophisticated, quantitative modern ecology where everything might appear to be already worked out. But countless ecological questions still arise that require answers, such as: How do you find them? How do you measure them? How do you even count them? Every species or every set of environmental interactions has a slightly different answer. The brush pile technique of catching turtles at night has had a major impact on the study of river turtles. Our approach to catching cooters will not be used by many herpetologists. But no biologist in the world can study an animal he or she cannot catch or find. Developing a method for collecting your study species is the first step in many ecological studies. Collecting techniques too often are taken for granted by some laboratory scientists who assume that animals come from biological supply houses. Plant ecologists probably do not appreciate the problem either. But herpetologists do, especially those who work with snakes. Finding out how to find snakes is an important step in studying them.

The traditional manner in which herpetologists, including those aged twelve or younger, collect snakes is simply to go into a habitat and look for them. One quickly learns that few snakes sit in plain view and await your arrival. Instead, most species in most places must be sought under boards or rocks or leaves or whatever else one can find to turn over. A snake collector definitely gets better at it through experience, by learning that certain weather conditions, seasons, habitats, and times of day are unsuitable whereas others are more likely to produce a higher yield. Even so, herpetologists with decades of experience behind them can go out snake collecting and come back empty-handed. Perhaps that's one of the appeals of the field—something like a day at the races, except that snakes are the purse and your time is the bet. If you are out snake collecting for a hobby, then catching a scarlet kingsnake is like winning the daily double. Catching a nasty water snake is like getting your money back. Anyway, walking through woods, along stream margins, up talus slopes, across prairies, or into swamps is all part of the oldest and most widespread means of collecting snakes, by finding and grabbing them.

The universality of this collecting approach extends to snake collectors of all types, from youngsters to professionals who collect snakes for a living, either for commercial purposes or for science. Although true professionals have their ways of being effective when large sample sizes or particular species are needed, the overall ineffectiveness of the technique, even though it is the best one, is distressing—one snake per hour! That's what we recently calculated on the basis of field notes of more than a dozen professional herpetologists. Most herpetologists themselves really have never considered the returns per time effort in this way because snake collecting is in one sense a sport. Deer or rabbit hunters would be absolutely ecstatic if they were to be so successful.

Another way to collect snakes, again with a bag score of about one specimen per hour, is road cruising. The ideal roads are blacktop, sparsely traveled ones in the right geographic region and during the right season. Most road collecting is done at night because most species of U.S. snakes are nocturnal and, in addition, this timing provides you with specimens of those forms you are not as likely to encounter during your daily activities.

Some of the best road collecting in the United States is in Florida and the Southwest. I have been on Alligator Alley, which connects Fort Meyers and Fort Lauderdale, Florida, and have seen, during a rainy period, as many as three hundred live snakes in one night. I also have been on Alligator Alley, all 150 miles of it, at night without seeing any reptiles, except for one Florida mud turtle. Likewise for west Texas. Once we collected thirty-two western diamondback rattlers plus numerous other snakes on sixty miles of highway late one evening in June 1961 only to return a month later and not see a single specimen. Road cruising is relaxing, if you're not worried about the gas, because you can have your coffee or whatever and can talk or listen to the radio. Essentially, road collecting is just a modernized, nighttime version of the original type of collecting on foot, but in a manner that assures you do not get too wet if it's raining.

Standard field collecting and road cruising are generalized approaches for catching snakes. As with any group of animals, certain species require specialty techniques that are most effective. Many people are aware of the south Georgia rattlesnake roundups. This modern gladiator sport preys on the lifestyles of two reptiles, one a turtle and the other the eastern diamondback rattlesnake.

Gopher tortoises are strictly terrestrial turtles of the southern United States, one species or another being found from Florida to California. The eastern variety lives in colonies in which the individual digs a burrow several feet into the ground to which it retreats at night or during cold weather. Rattlesnakes and gopher tortoises are compatible creatures paying no attention to one another except that the rattlers use the tortoise burrows in which to overwinter. The tortoises seem not to mind. Unfortunately, certain humans who care little for tortoises and even less for rattlesnakes have found a way to drive the rattlers out of the ground.

By using a plastic or rubber hose attached to a gasoline can, these people force fumes into the burrow during the late fall or winter (which is never very cold in southern Georgia). Although the snakes are dormant, they are not too cold to be active enough to leave the burrow and be caught as trophies during the rattlesnake roundups. The fate of the tortoises at the bottom of the burrow, or of the many other snakes, lizards, and mammals that share the communal hiding place, is uncertain in many instances. Nonetheless, gassing burrows is representative of how a specialty technique can be used if some critical part of an animal's life history is understood.

To Catch a Cooter • 111

Ecologists on the Savannah River Plant remove reptiles and amphibians from one of the more than one thousand pitfall traps used in studies of overland movement patterns of animals. More than five miles of drift fences have been installed at critical sites and more than 500,000 small vertebrates have been collected since the studies began in the late 1960s. Many of them have been rare or seldom-seen species such as star-nosed moles and rainbow snakes.

No matter what environmental questions an ecologist wishes to answer, the first problem is to obtain an adequate sample of the organisms being studied. Collecting methods vary from one species to the next and often require an element of ingenuity on the part of the investigator. As seen in the previous chapters, the means of collecting various types of reptiles and amphibians have been a major part of the study effort.

But in herpetology only one technique besides hand collecting and road collecting has proved to be effective for a wide range of species in an area. In fact, the drift fence with pitfall traps may have caught greater numbers and more species of reptiles and amphibians than any other trapping technique used in herpetology. Although we did not invent the drift fence on the SRP, we definitely have capitalized on the technique.

Few places in the United States could be more ideally suited for the drift fence technique than the SRP in South Carolina. The SRP combines a wealth of reptile and amphibian species with complete protection for research equipment left in the field. Vandalism, the scourge of field ecologists in most areas of the United States, is nonexistent on the SRP. All we have to worry about is an occasional wayward alligator or a wild boar who decides to go over, or through, the fence.

Our drift fences are made from thirty-inch-high aluminum flashing sunk about six inches beneath the soil to prevent smaller animals from burrowing under. Five-gallon buckets that we call pitfall traps are buried along each side of the fence at thirty-foot intervals. The open ends of the buckets are flush with the ground and abut the fence. When small overland travelers such as insects, frogs, salamanders, snakes, turtles, mice, and rats encounter the fence, they follow it and fall into the bucket. Seldom-seen species that live beneath the leaf litter may run into the underground portion of the fence, surface for a short distance, and also end up in a bucket. Poor jumpers or climbers remain captive until the daily trap check. Our longest drift fence completely encircles a natural wetland area, a Carolina bay known as Ellenton Bay; the fence is almost a mile long and has 246 buckets.

Drift fences have taught us a lot about the ecology of animals. And one of the most dramatic of these lessons is that our natural environments are still teeming with a wide variety of creatures that most people never see. For example, throughout most of its range in the Southeast the rainbow snake is seldom seen and is regarded by many herpetologists as one of the rarest and most beautiful snakes. I know professional herpetologists who have never seen one in the wild. Yet, I recall Easter Sunday 1975 when Tom Murphy, John Coker, and I checked the drift fence at Ellenton Bay and caught twenty-eight, perhaps the largest sample ever collected on a single day.

Small mammals are another example. The star-nosed mole looks and acts strangely by most standards. A peculiar-looking attachment on the end of its nose resembles a star with twenty points. The points are tentacles used to search for food. This mole spends a major portion of its time foraging underwater. Predominantly a northern species, very few star-nosed moles ever had been reported in the South before the construction of our drift fences. Despite intensive trapping efforts by conventional means in the past century, star-nosed moles had been reported from fewer than ten localities in South Carolina and only two specimens had been found in Georgia by the 1960s.

We caught our first star-nosed mole in 1969, about three months after installing our drift fences in South Carolina, a few miles from the Georgia border. Since then we've captured more than a dozen from five different localities. We soon will have more specimens from the region than were caught in both states combined over the previous century. Star-nosed moles are probably not so rare in the Carolinas and Georgia, except from the perspective of those who have not been able to catch them, thus indicating the value and importance of using the right technique.

A similar situation has occurred with a tiny insect-eating mammal known as the southeastern shrew. Shrews are the smallest mammals in the world, and the southeastern shrew is among the tiniest of its kind. Were you to try to trap a southeastern shrew, you would understand how one might think them to be exceedingly rare. Most previous reports of the species came from specimens that house cats had dropped at someone's feet. Because of its presumed rarity a group of mammalogists recently proposed this animal for endangered species status in South Carolina. But drift fences revealed that these shrews are not rare at all. They just happen to be very secretive and have an aversion to going into conventional mammal traps. However, when they are burrowing beneath the soil and leaf litter and encounter the buried part of a drift fence they come to the surface and follow the fence until they fall into a bucket. Like the star-nosed mole, the little brown shrews with the long, funny noses are not rare, just secretive and usually uncatchable, unless you use the proper technique.

Besides revealing "what's there?" the drift fence technique also can be used to study the functional ecology of animals. For example, a species' primary direction of movement during a particular period of time is revealed by whether individuals are captured most frequently in the inside or outside buckets along the fence. In some studies a reliable estimate can be made of what the net exchange between two habitats is based on the entry and exit of the individuals of each species. The information on the movement by different species can be complemented with studies to determine the concentrations of critical chemical elements in the individuals of each species. No single species is going to significantly change the balance of minerals and nutrients in a habitat, but collectively the small mammals, reptiles, and amphibians may prove to be important. Furthermore, such research contributes to our understanding of how animals redistribute chemical elements in natural environments.

The most instructive life history data collected to date with the drift fence technique have been with turtles and amphibians. Frogs and salamanders are ideal research subjects for the drift fence and pitfall trap approach. Most of them plod or hop along with staunch purpose toward aquatic breeding areas during some given season of the year, depending on the species. For most forms of amphibians the first step in the basic life cycle is to mate and lay eggs in an aquatic habitat (usually a temporary, rain-filled basin where fish are least likely to occur). Within a few days or weeks the eggs hatch into aquatic larvae or tadpoles, metamorphose, and then move onto land to carry out their mature lives. Thus, the adults return to the terrestrial environment (which may be hundreds of yards from the water) and their routine existence until next year's breeding period. The questions facing a field ecologist about the amphibian assemblages at a habitat are those such as: How many individuals of each species depend on the habitat? When are the critical periods of overland migration? Where do the animals come from? These and many other ecological questions are answerable with (some of them *only* with) the drift fence technique.

The importance of amphibians as predominant prey species in a region is documented by some of the numbers of such organisms captured on the SRP. The record for numbers probably belongs to the eastern leopard frogs captured at a small Carolina bay known as Rainbow Bay. During 1979 a total of 25,000 specimens of this species was collected at a 1,400-foot drift fence that encircles the aquatic area. This number represents an average of more than three individual frogs for each inch of fence around the aquatic area! The highest record for a single day was more than 5,000 leopard frogs. No standard herpetological collecting technique ever could have revealed the overwhelmingly high abundance of this species in the region.

Similarly, high and unsuspected numbers of the eastern mole salamander were revealed by the technique, but in this case additional information was learned about their functional ecology. Karen Patterson used the drift fences and pitfall traps on the SRP to demonstrate a previously unknown feature of the mole salamander's life history. That is, the larvae behaved differently in different aquatic habitats, depending upon the changes in water level. In Ellenton Bay, one of the largest and deepest Carolina bays, about three thousand adults came in to breed each fall and winter. However, rather than metamorphosing and emerging onto land in the following spring or summer as they did in the smaller Carolina bays, many of them kept their gills, stayed in the water, and matured as larvae. The phenomenon had been reported to occur with other types of salamanders but not under the habitat conditions at Ellenton Bay. The drift fence technique permitted Karen to quantify the amount and timing of the entry and exit of salamanders under differing environmental conditions and therefore to understand better the ecological processes that were in operation.

Drift fences have aided in "oh my" ecological revelations for a variety of animal groups. But the most thorough studies have been done with aquatic turtles that, as the drift fences have shown us, have a penchant for being terrestrial. Drift fences have provided turtle researchers with some of the basic, standard information needed by population ecologists. Egg laying, overland movement

Albinism is of rare occurrence in all wild animals but can occur in any species. This albino eastern mud turtle, the only one ever found, was collected in a pitfall trap as it entered Ellenton Bay, a freshwater habitat on the Savannah River Plant. Had it not been collected that day, it is doubtful that the individual would have survived very long because of its vulnerability to predation.

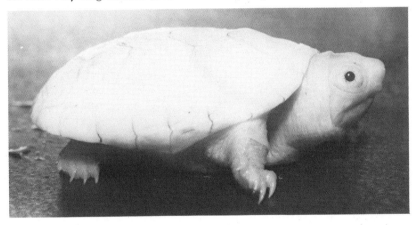

by turtles between different aquatic habitats, entry by hatchling turtles from the nest to the water—to accomplish any of these acts, a turtle must move between the water and land interface, the zone where we set up our drift fences and pitfall traps; thus, we can find out when and how often a particular event occurs. Besides gathering a foundation of necessary demographic and behavioral data, drift fences have permitted us to obtain the answers to certain specific questions about turtle ecology. One of these was a phenomenon we observed about eastern mud turtles, as revealed in Chapter 9.

CHAPTER 9

More Techniques:

To Find a Mud Turtle

I still remember the day we discovered where the eastern mud turtle spends the winter. Dave Bennett, Chris Franson, and I were riding across an abandoned cotton field in a government jeep. Dave drove while Chris and I watched the dial and listened to the Geiger counter. The long boom with the sodium iodide crystal extended out from the back of the jeep.

We all looked discouraged, and Chris and I looked dusty. Sitting on the tailgate while riding across abandoned cotton fields in South Carolina after a month of little rain is expected to be dusty. So we were not discouraged about that. But we had yet to locate any of the radioactive tantalum tags we had placed on the turtles several days before. Dave reached the edge of the 500-acre field and turned the jeep around as we shifted our survey to another section of the field.

We were attempting to solve a biological mystery of which our drift fences had made us aware. Each autumn, as the weather cooled, our pitfall traps captured large numbers of mud turtles as they moved out onto land away from the aquatic areas where they spend the spring and summer. Strange behavior for an aquatic turtle, we thought. One idea was that they were going to other (larger?) bodies of water to spend the winter. But the drift fence and pitfall traps at Ellenton Bay revealed that the mud turtles left the aquatic habitat there in all directions, not in any particular one. Some of the turtles clearly were not headed toward any other body of water. Furthermore, the closest lake that was any larger than Ellenton Bay was miles away. The same individuals returned each spring, so they were obviously safe for their half a year away from their summer home. Where did they go?

A capsule containing thread that will unravel when pulled is placed on the back of a turtle as one means of relocating an individual of a species once it has been captured. The thread trailer allows herpetologists to obtain information about an animal's movement patterns, which would be difficult to learn without continual observation over a long period of time. Because most turtles are reluctant to carry out normal activities when someone is watching, the trailer technique permits the investigator to release an animal and come back the following day to find out where it traveled by simply following the trail left by the thread.

When we decided to use the tantalum tag technique, we did not know if it would work at all. Radioactive tags had been used as location devices for other animals, though, so the concept was logical. In an early study with box turtles—in which the question was, "Where do they go?"—Dr. Lucille Stickel in Maryland had used a spool of thread attached to the backs of turtles to determine where they spent their time. The thread unwound as the turtle plodded around in its home range, and the next day the ecologist could come back and leisurely map out the turtle's movement pattern. I think of this as the "classical approach." We have tried putting such thread trailers on the backs of the departing turtles captured at the Ellenton Bay drift fence, but the habitat in which we had chosen to work prevented us from being successful, for the vegetation zone closest to the water was blackberry bushes.

The pleasure derived from blackberries in a bowl or in a pie in no way compensates for the misery one receives from working around the bushes. Blackberry bushes behave as a thinking predator when you walk by. If one, just one, tiny brier catches your shirt sleeve, then the whole prickly branch is pulled toward you. Blackberry bushes are particularly effective at catching you in early fall when the thorns are longest and stiffest but the branches are still supple. Until you have gained enough experience to know to stop dead in your tracks when a bush catches you, your natural response is to pull away. This movement raises the ire of the whole bush, so that all of the branches reach out to embrace you. This action also engages two or three other bushes whose branches are intertwined with the first one. I suppose if the branches were long enough you soon would be involved with every blackberry bush in the vicinity. I can't honestly say that blackberry bushes will actually drag a man in and devour him, but Joab Thomas tells of an event that happened when he was a botanist at Harvard that might make you think they could.

Joab and a colleague were on a field trip in Cuba where a plant called catclaw grows. Although blackberry bushes and catclaw are not closely related botanically, from a zoologist's standpoint they are simply regional versions of aggravation for the field ecologist. Both behave similarly when it comes to grabbing you and holding on with little hooks and spines.

Joab's companion was a botanist interested in orchids, many species of which grow in Cuba. But, an orchid known as *Eulophia ecristata* is uncommon, even there, so when they saw one shyly standing alone a few feet into a massive catclaw thicket, nothing would do but to collect it for the Gray Herbarium at Harvard.

Joab watched while his botanist companion maneuvered his way under the catclaw briers, carefully removing each barbed sticker in turn, so that none of the branches and bushes grabbed him. The orchid was finally within arm's reach as he lay outstretched beneath the catclaw patch. He yanked the little orchid plant out of the ground, and simultaneously added his first *Eulophia ecristata* and his first disturbed yellow jacket nest to his list of lifetime experiences in ecology. Needless to say the catclaw bushes did all they could to keep him from escaping as the flying devils poured out of the hole beside the orchid's roots. The orchid died on the ground somewhere beneath the bushes, the botanist was hospitalized, and the yellow jackets had to repair their nest. But the catclaw bushes went along unaffected, except for the tiny pieces of cloth and skin on a good many stickers. The blackberry bushes we deal with would have done the same thing had they been there.

Anyway, back in South Carolina, few of our turtles were ever able to make it through the blackberry bushes at our study site without breaking the trailer string or actually having the trailer pulled off. The turtles did fine until they encountered the twenty- to fifty-foot-wide blackberry bush zone that margined the aquatic area. Under the circumstances, the thread trailer technique was not effective for following the movement patterns of turtles.

Because our objective was simply to find the turtle later, not have its exact route laid out by a piece of string, we considered using radios as locating devices. But eastern mud turtles do not get much larger than a man's fist and at that time, the late 1960s, radiotelemetry was not refined to the point of being used with efficiency on a small animal. So, we moved toward the idea of using a radioactive isotope that could be placed on or in the animal without harming it but that would emit sufficient gamma radiation to permit detection from several feet away. Tantalum-182 was the isotope we chose. A piece of tantalum wire the diameter of a paper clip and about one-quarter of an inch in length sufficed for locating a turtle twenty-five to thirty feet away.

Turtles proved to be ideal subjects for such studies, too. First, they have been shown to be very resistant to radiation damage, more so, in fact, than practically any other vertebrate examined experimentally. Second, the tag could be quickly and safely placed in the turtle. We simply drilled a tiny hole into the back edge of the shell, dropped the radioactive pin into it, and put Duco cement on top of the hole. Within minutes we could have a field-caught turtle outfitted with a radioactive location device and have it released at the site of capture.

We outfitted and released a dozen turtles that were leaving our aquatic study area during September. Upon release, each turtle, after a one- to two-hour wait, finally would crawl under the closest leaf litter and sit. The study had not revealed anything up till that day that Chris and Dave and I were in the jeep, as none of the turtles had moved more than three feet from where they were first released following implantation of the tantalum pins. But that day was different. That day eight of the ten turtles *had* moved from their release points. But where? Had they gone to other aquatic habitats? The river swamp? Presumably some environmental change, such as the preceding balmy day followed with the light rain and a cooler temperature, had cued their response to leave. They were definitely gone from where each had been two days before.

Sitting in the jeep, we were now more than one hundred yards from the water and only one hundred feet from the woods when we started back across the field. Each fifty feet we moved out meant a bigger area had to be covered. Increasing discouragement was to be expected.

Chris and I both started as the Geiger counter crackled for a moment and then stopped. We yelled for Dave to back up the jeep. Sure enough, as he backed up, we reached a point where the static was louder and steadier than that caused by natural background radiation. Under normal background the counter will have erratic but ephemeral bursts. This static was a continual crackle. The sound became louder as we jumped down and waved the boom over the ground. The sound came from the sandy section in the field about twenty feet from the jeep. We closed in.

A few minutes later we were reading the code written in white enamel paint on the back of a male mud turtle we had released six days before. We had to scratch away an inch of sand and ground litter to see the top of the shell where the numbers were written. We put the sand back so as not to disturb the turtle.

The remainder of the afternoon yielded five more of the eight missing turtles. Each was buried about an inch beneath the soil somewhere out in the old field. One of them was more than half a mile away from its release point alongside the drift fence. I felt

To Find a Mud Turtle • 123

good about the study from that day on and into the next spring when all six of these turtles, as well as several others that we located later, returned to the Ellenton Bay aquatic habitat from which they had come. We kept a record of where each stayed during the fall and winter and found they did not move much. They just remained buried beneath the surface and responded to unduly cold weather by burrowing a little deeper.

The radioactive tagging technique was invaluable to verify that mud turtles hibernate on land. We had suspected the possibility from our terrestrial drift fence records but the tracking technique had permitted us to find out for sure. Drift fences and radioactive tags also have been used in concert in other studies on the SRP. The use of radioactive tantalum pins inserted into the tails of salamanders captured in pitfall traps as they left the aquatic sites allowed Ray Semlitsch to determine where adult mole salamanders go on land. Ray was able to track the overland movements of individuals that were leaving the breeding habitat. The use of a radioactive tag as a detectable marker in the field can provide superlative information about a small, secretive salamander. Ray found that most of the animals he followed traveled up to three hundred feet from the aquatic habitat, remained underground, and occupied only a few square feet throughout the entire summer. This information attests to the difficulty in studying such creatures and also explains why we have impressions that such animals are less common than they really are.

Unusual techniques have been the salvation of innumerable life history studies of plants and animals because each species has its own biological personality that must be considered in designing a technique to study it. For safety reasons, most ecologists do not conduct research in areas that would permit free-ranging radioisotopes. But another technique, radiotelemetry, has become important to animal ecologists everywhere.

A radio or sonic transmitter attached to a particular specimen allows ecologists to determine its location and follow its movement throughout the year. The use of the most sophisticated equipment even permits investigators to monitor the physiological responses of an animal to environmental conditions. Recent studies on free-ranging alligators have used probes attached at selected regions of the body to monitor physiological and environmental characteris-

One means of locating turtles, particularly those moving long distances, is the use of radio transmitters attached to their shells. A transmitter and battery pack are encased in waterproof plastic and glued to a turtle's shell. Earphones and a receiving antenna permit the investigator to locate the exact position of the animal underwater in large lakes or rivers. In one study conducted along a river, Dr. Michael Plummer tracked soft-shell turtles more than seven miles in this manner.

tics. Rate of heart beat, surface or internal body temperature, depth of the alligator in the water, and other important information can be telemetered to researchers more than a mile away. Electronics has become a powerful tool of field ecologists.

Knowledge of daily and seasonal movement patterns is vital to understanding the total ecology of an animal. Yet, these critical data can be very difficult to obtain. In the situation in South Carolina where one end of the large Par Pond reservoir is warmed by water from a nuclear reactor, such information is particularly relevant. Ecologists of the region have observed an unusual phenomenon with American alligators. During winter, when the alligators are normally dormant, large adults in the population were observed routinely in the heated portion of the lake. An extensive study on the movement patterns of the alligators in response to the warm water was conducted by Tom Murphy and Dr. I. Lehr Brisbin of SREL. Several large alligators were collected from the reservoir and then released following the attachment of neck collars in which tiny transmitters were embedded.

The signal from a transmitter is amplified by a hand-held receiving unit and is detectable to the investigator through earphones or directly from the unit itself. By recording the movement of the transmittered animals and making additional observations in the reservoir, the ecologists concluded that the large, male alligators moved from cooler regions of the lake into the artificially heated portions. Although the males moved to the heated area in December and remained there, actively feeding, throughout the winter, the juveniles and most females remained dormant in the cooler sections of the lake.

The elevated water temperatures also alter the spring movement patterns of the alligators, affecting their reproductive behavior. Male alligators residing in warm temperature areas during winter have sperm present in the penile groove as much as four weeks earlier than normal and therefore may not be in breeding synchrony with females in the population, according to the studies of Murphy and Brisbin. Additional studies are under way to explain why only the males appear to become reproductively active early in response to the elevated temperatures.

Because of the difficulty in making observations on wild animals, an understanding of the movement patterns and potential impact on the population ecology of the alligators would have been almost impossible without radiotelemetry. Radiotelemetry also has allowed insight into the seemingly simple but intriguingly complex question of why turtles bask in the sun. Do turtles bask merely to warm up? The question has far-reaching implications in understanding how reptiles and other cold-blooded animals control their body temperature. Thermoregulation is vital to the well-being of an organism. As turtles are the epitome of sun bathers, ecologists have made numerous studies to determine the primary purpose of the simple sun-basking habit. Elevating body temperature is only one explanation scientists have given for why turtles bask. Other explanations include drying up external parasites and algae, fulfilling vitamin requirements, or just plain resting.

Research with turtles carrying temperature-sensitive radiotelemetry probes has elucidated some of the mechanisms and complexities of thermoregulation in reptiles. Research by Jim Spotila and Ed Standora has shown that experimental turtles carrying transmitters in the warm portion of the Par Pond reservoir do not leave the water to bask, even on cool sunny days. However, on the same days, transmittered turtles in the cool sections of the same lake routinely bask. In addition, when the artificially heated reservoir becomes too warm, those turtles that do not leave the warm section of the lake burrow into the mud where temperatures are much cooler. The transmitters revealed that, whatever the environment, the turtles managed to maintain their preferred body temperatures (around 82°F. in the summertime) by basking, burrowing, or taking advantage of the heated effluent when possible.

Continuing research with telemetry has revealed that turtles can precisely control body temperature by adjusting for water temperature, amount of exposure to sunlight, wind speed, relative humidity, and other environmental factors. Hence, in natural environments turtles maintain their body temperatures at optimal levels by carefully determining the length of time they bask. Although many aspects of this facet of animal ecology remain unexplored and unexplained at this time, the recent advances in biotelemetry have allowed us to probe far deeper than ever before. Continued ecological research using these newly developed electronic techniques can only lead to more fascinating and exciting discoveries.

Sometimes a useful technique in ecology may seem innovative and imaginative whereas actually the idea has been used for years in another profession. Pitfall traps were used centuries ago by primitive people in search of an efficient way to capture large game. Electronics has been used for decades by the military as a tracking and sensing device. Likewise, the medical profession has had its impact on herpetology and ecology.

The dissection of animals is frequently a necessary step in medical research. In some ecological studies, dissection is the only way to obtain valuable information on certain aspects of a species' life history. However, when animal ecologists study rare species or medical doctors look inside humans, the sacrifice of even one or a few specimens may be excessive. Or, if a population of a common species is studied for a long time, each specimen may develop an intrinsic value to the scientist so that its dissection and death would not be desirable. How do we study animals that cannot be dissected?

The solution to the dilemma varies with the species. Sometimes no known method, using even the most modern techniques, will permit certain information to be obtained without sacrificing the animal. For example, how can an ichthyologist determine what an anglerfish eats without harming the animal? Some anglerfish live more than two miles deep in the ocean and literally explode when brought to the surface. No simple technique has been devised to deal with this problem. But for some animals, techniques to displace dissection are being devised. The following examples are based on some of the work conducted on freshwater turtles at SREL.

In research involving industrial or other human-caused impacts to the environment, turtles are often the study species. The reasons are several. They are hardy, can tolerate excessive industrial or domestic pollution, and live for long periods of time. Thus, long-term effects of pollution can be examined.

However, a paradox situation arises. Should the ecologist collect long-term information on individuals without sacrificing any of them? Or should some portion of the study population be destroyed each year to gain information obtainable only by dissection? Using common medical techniques, we have successfully solved the problem of whether to dissect part of a study population for two important facets of turtle ecology—diet and reproduction.

Food habits must be known in order to understand the intricate energetic relationships among plants and animals. Heretofore, most ecological studies have depended upon dissection of specimens and examination of their stomach contents to determine the diet of a species or population. We now use a technique that spares the turtle's life yet reveals what the animal eats. Although the specimen is subjected to a bit of indignity, the method is harmless and the animal can be released with everything (except its previous

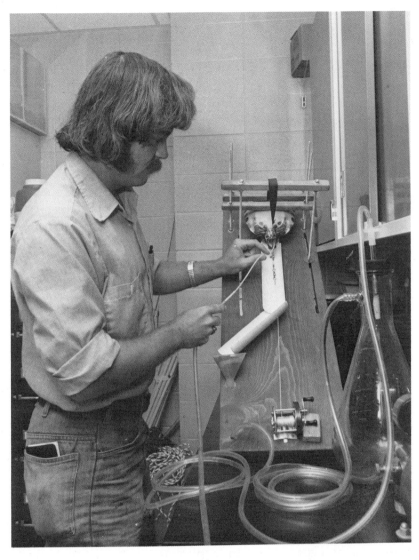

The turtle dietometer allows herpetologists to determine what the animals are eating without eliminating the individual from the study population. The device, designed by Bob Parmenter, uses the technique of flushing out the turtle's stomach with water while the mouth is held open.

meal) intact. The principle is based on flushing out the turtle's stomach with water in a manner similar to that used with humans in hospitals.

A restraining device for holding the specimen's mouth open and keeping the long neck straight was developed by Bob Parmenter, a graduate student at the University of Georgia. A small tube is inserted through the turtle's mouth to the stomach. A steady stream of water then is forced into the stomach so that all contents are disgorged. Coincidentally, a similar approach was presented recently by Dr. John Legler of the University of Utah. He developed the technique in Australia, where turtles are not common and the protection of individual specimens is important. Presumably the stomach pump method can be extended to other groups of animals for which we have no harmless methods for obtaining dietary information.

Information about animal reproductive patterns is also ecologically important. For example, certain environmental conditions may not appear to affect the individuals of a species; but, if reproduction has been altered in some critical manner, such as increasing or decreasing the average number of eggs, then the effect is obviously an important one. For many animal species this situation means that females must be dissected at critical periods to determine how many young would have been born or how many eggs were to be laid.

To avoid the problem of dissecting female sea turtles, Dr. Archie Carr and his associates at the University of Florida have gathered vast amounts of information on nesting behavior and other aspects of egg laying by patrolling ocean beaches at night in search of female sea turtles leaving the water. If she is allowed to start digging the nest undisturbed, a sea turtle usually will complete the egg-laying process even when an audience is gathered around counting the eggs as they are deposited.

Although successfully employed for sea turtles, the direct observation technique has not been used effectively with the species of freshwater turtles in the United States. Females of most freshwater species are difficult to locate while depositing eggs, because they normally do not emerge onto an open beach with no vegetation to conceal them, the way sea turtles do. However, most can be captured by setting traps in the aquatic habitat several days prior to

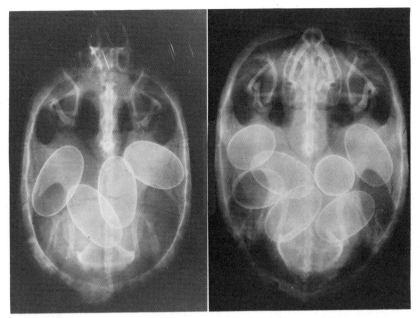

X-ray photography is used at the Savannah River Ecology Lab to reveal egg number in a freshwater turtle. The technique does not appear to harm the female or the hatchlings. X-ray photography of females can be employed successfully with any egg-laying reptile and should provide opportunities to address heretofore unanswered questions in reproductive ecology.

egg laying, when the full complement of eggs is contained in the oviducts. Or, if a drift fence with pitfall traps is used, females can be captured on their way to nesting sites. Reproductive information is of importance in our studies, yet we do not want to kill and dissect the animals. With the help of Judy Greene, SREL research assistant, and the cooperation of local medical technicians, we attempted a new approach with turtles—X-ray photography. And it worked.

Use of the X-ray technique became widespread in the mid-1970s after a scientific publication revealed how useful X-rays could be in determining egg numbers in turtles. The importance of X-ray photography is that scientists now can determine how many eggs a turtle or other reptile is going to lay without having to kill and dissect the female—the old-fashioned method. The field of herpetology, not to mention the reptiles and amphibians themselves, has benefited greatly from the use of the technique by ecologists who study reproductive output in the animals. No longer is it necessary to destructively sample a population by killing females to determine the size of the clutches.

Since 1975, with the use of X-ray photography, we have determined egg production in more than five hundred female turtles who suffered only minor inconvenience in making their contributions to science. We also performed experiments to see if baby turtles raised from X-rayed eggs suffered undue mortality or mutation. The results: X-rayed young were normal and hatched in the same proportion as natural eggs. We also have made sufficient preliminary observations on egg-laying snakes and lizards to assure that the technique will be effective with other reptile groups. A recent series of X-ray photographs on water snakes and cottonmouth moccasins even has shown that the method can be used to determine litter size in species that do not lay eggs.

A recent use of X-ray photography was instituted in the study of a group of water snakes. Among snakes, the skull bone shape, bone sizes, and patterns of alignment are key characters in determining the relationship of different species. In earlier studies it was necessary to prepare a complete skeleton including the skull for comparative purposes. Not only is the skeleton preparation technique time consuming but it results in destructive sampling of snake populations. Recently it was discovered that many of these key skull characters are readily seen on X-ray photographs so that not only can live specimens be used and then released but also a much larger number of animals can be examined in a study. Clearly this procedure is an advantage in the study of rare or endangered species in which the loss of a single specimen may not be permissible.

Another use of X-ray photography has been to examine abnormalities that appear in the bone structure or, in the case of turtles, the shells without having the onerous task of specimen preparation. For example, whether additional limbs or digits are present because of bone abnormalities or simply because of abnormal muscle or skin development can be determined easily with an X-ray. Such information may be useful in interpreting the causes and consequences of various forms of environmental or genetic problems.

X-rays depend predominantly on calcium deposits, such as those in eggs or bones, and therefore have been very useful for studies dealing with these structures. A recent advance has shown that even embryos in live-bearing snakes can be counted near the end of parturition so that litter counts can be made without dissecting the female. These and other uses of X-ray technology already have led to advances in understanding herpetology and permits herpetologists to proceed in the spirit of modern-day efforts to preserve natural populations of animals whenever possible.

The development of techniques in herpetology or any field of science is an endless exercise, for as long as new questions arise we must have new approaches to find the answers. In field herpetology the first technique may be as basic as an ingenious method of finding and catching the study species. Some techniques will track technological advances, although the application to a specific field may not be forthcoming for many years. Answering questions that help understand the biology of plants and animals is the primary challenge of ecologists, but finding exactly the right technique to get an answer can be a gratifying and critical challenge in itself and always will be appreciated by the scientists who follow.

CHAPTER 10

The Future of Reptiles and Amphibians:

Can We Find a Hiding Place, Too?

The beam from my headlight picked up the yellow chin, held aloof and arrogant above the black swamp mud. Cottonmouth moccasins either know they are poisonous or at least know they are special in some way—because every one you see, whether coiled on a rotting cypress stump or crossing a logging road through a southern swamp, holds its head up, proudly. I always say that you're safer from cottonmouths in the swamp at night (with a light) than in the day. Their chins reflect even the dimmest light and make them easy to spot.

We caught this one by hand as we always do and put it into the sack with the other two. I argue with certain other herpetologists about whether it's safer to pick up snakes by hand than mess around with snake tongs. You lose a few snakes with tongs, either by injuring them or letting them escape. Hand holding a pit viper behind the head, finger and thumb firmly pushed against the rear portion of the poison glands, is the sure way. I always use my left hand, though, to play safe.

Catching cottonmouths is a pretty straightforward endeavor for a snake collector down South. They're fairly predictable about the habitats in which you might find them, the seasons and times of day they're likely to be active, and the type of behavior they're going to display. That night, my knowledge of cottonmouths revealed the depth of my (and other people's) ignorance about a particular environment—for after catching the three cottonmouths in the Savannah River swamp, we drove to another site, a place that I had assumed would be excellent for finding plenty of cottonmouths and nonpoisonous water snakes.

All of us in the jeep that night, as we drove out of the swamp, considered ourselves true ecologists—involved in, dedicated to, immersed in the study of the environment. And because we were also herpetologists we assumed that we knew a lot about snakes, especially poisonous cottonmouths and harmless water snakes. We drove with a mission, from the swamp to the reservoir, ready to make a major haul along the margins of the big lake. Any southern herpetologist knows you can catch snakes easily from a boat if you patrol the banks of a southern reservoir at night. We enjoyed the bliss of our ignorance during the fifteen-minute jeep ride. The 2½-hour boat ride that followed was one of the most disappointing field trips, from the standpoint of snake collecting, that I have taken.

No one knew much about the ecology of the Par Pond reservoir in 1968. What is today the most-studied thermal reservoir in the world was a black box of environmental mystery to the local ecologists at that time. Comparatively few trips had been made onto the lake by biologists. Most sampling had been done by limnologists or health physicists taking water samples. How was I to know that Par Pond's snakes were different from those anywhere else I had been?

Surely any herpetologist who worked with snakes would have expected to find them along the banks of Par Pond that night. The reactor was on, pouring millions of gallons of unmercifully hot water into the far end of the reservoir, a mile away. By the time the waters reached midlake they had cooled considerably, but they elevated the upper reaches of the reservoir a few degrees above normal temperatures—not a lethal level, but a mild, lukewarm bath. At that time I thought any reptile would be too impressed to leave.

We drifted through the mist, using the outboard along the long, open shores and paddling back into the coves. The shifting head-light beams reminded one of a prison escape as we searched the water-land interface, the open water, the overhanging branches, and the shore for cottonmouths or water snakes. None was to be found. We continued, covering unexplored parts of the reservoir. Dangling a hand overboard I could feel the thermal change as we moved from warm to cool and back. I was most impressed. Not a snake in two and a half hours! A record for a warm spring night in South Carolina.

I felt wiser as we pulled away in the jeep from the shoreline area we defined as a boat landing. Driving back to the lab I marveled at

Can We Find a Hiding Place, Too? • 135

the absolute lack of snakes in the reservoir and reached the obvious conclusion that the bizarre conditions were responsible. The snakes could not make the necessary thermoregulatory adjustments, I assumed.

But a little learning had indeed not helped. Par Pond, the most magnificent thermal reservoir in the country, had few snakes, to be sure. But thermoregulation was not the answer. Ironically, we had observed the answer that very night many times, but we had been too naive to recognize it. Far more important to the snakes than water temperature per se were the powerful jaws that lay in the water in front of the dozens of pairs of bright red eyes that we had seen. It was in fact many years later before I was satisfied with the observation that when alligators hold the franchise on a sparsely vegetated aquatic habitat, snakes are rarely seen. A surface swimming snake has no chance when a hungry alligator is near. And Par Pond, as was later reinforced to us with the turtle traps, was full of alligators.

Over the years, Par Pond revealed our ignorance about environmental phenomena of many types, many times. We learned much over the next few months and, if no other general teaching emerges, we all can say that we learned how ignorant we sometimes can be without even being aware that we do not know.

That night, while snakes in the vicinity of Par Pond had to deal with the threat of alligators, snakes and other animals throughout the region faced another problem, as exemplified in the following scenario:

A tiny head nudged aside the blades of grass alongside the road shoulder, waited a moment, and then the creature proceeded onto the blacktop highway. It crossed the center stripe before the headlights approaching from the creek bottom were even visible. As the truck thundered up the highway onto the sandhill plateau, the animal paused, the natural response by some species when danger is imminent. The response was not necessarily to sound as we know it, for snakes have no middle ear, but instead may have been to other cues, perhaps to the sudden light in the midnight darkness or to ground vibrations.

As the truck roared past, along the turkey oak–bordered highway, the scarlet snake's flattened body lay motionless except for the rhythmically twitching tail that marks the final minutes of a

Few children are afraid of snakes until they are taught to be by adults. Unfortunately, most people learn to fear snakes rather than to respect them so that the many varieties of harmless snakes are not fully appreciated by most people. Some snakes make good pets, if you accept them for what they are.

dying snake. When the morning sun cleared the tallest cypresses and struck the hilltop, the little snake's bright red, white, and black–patterned body gave evidence that in the Southeast snakes are a major prey of America's most unwitting predator, the automobile.

The carcass of a large canebrake rattler lay a few hundred feet down the hill at the swamp's margin. The skid marks across its body and its missing rattles attested that it had died from the same "predator." But the driver had seen this snake, swerved into the wrong lane, and hit the brakes in order to skid over the body. The rattles had made a nice trophy.

Thus, snakes, as well as other animals and plants and entire natural ecosystems, die today from a combination of disinterest and design. Without question, snakes and every other living thing die constantly from natural causes. But the process has been slow and methodical and has not proceeded at the breathtaking rate of our present-day style of progress. Under natural conditions, species have time to adapt and coadapt and adjust to the gradual changes, an unaffordable luxury in today's world of overnight environmental overhaul. But the issues of what to do and who's at fault are endless. Sometimes a particular species such as a snail darter or the whooping crane can serve to focus our attention on particular issues or philosophical attitudes. The final conclusion is that agreement among the parties often can be as rare as the animal under discussion. To address the dilemma of special species and how we are to deal with them, I offer a reptile, the indigo snake, as the paragon of paradox in demonstrating why environmentalists and developers and professional ecologists and industrialists and farmers and anyone else who cares about the presence of the environment, for one reason or another, frequently cannot come to terms with each other.

Okefenokee Joe is what Dick Flood, former curator of animals at the Okefenokee Swamp Park, calls himself. Okefenokee Joe and I are kindred. We both like snakes and want what's best for them. We like places where lots of snakes live and we dislike activities that disrupt the lives of the snakes that live there. Although I haven't asked him, we probably both hold deep respect and admiration for seven-foot-long diamondback rattlesnakes, a foot in circumference. And neither of us would want to see you kill one that size. If you told us how dangerous it was, we would tell you that the 220-volt wire to your clothes dryer is far deadlier. But you have been taught that 220-volt wires are not dangerous if you handle them properly or don't handle them at all. We all accept that high voltage wires have a place in our society. Rattlesnakes also have a place in our environment. Okefenokee Joe and I both would agree that to alter their being is as presumptuous as to remove electrical wiring from people's houses.

But Okefenokee Joe and I do not agree on how to protect such animals. I believe that the official designation of a species as "endangered" or "threatened" can have positive effects on the survival of that species. Legislation attracts public attention in the same way that a snake does in front of an audience. I think the strategy is a good one but Okefenokee Joe has, in contrast, some very thought-provoking comments in the following, slightly modified and abstracted version of his letter to the state of Georgia when the indigo snake was under consideration as an endangered species in that state.

10 January 1977

Dear Sir:

Because I care about all wildlife, I must at this time express my views regarding the status of the indigo snake in the state of Georgia. I have spent many hours in the outlying areas of southeastern Georgia studying the activities of certain animals, among them the indigo, checking out theories, and pondering the eventual outcome of man's constant and relentless intervention into the all too delicate balance of this cycle. I know the indigo well, probably better than anyone in this state. He is beautiful, magnificent, and totally beneficial to man, and yet, with all due respect to those who wish him protected, I believe that placing the indigo snake on the endangered species list in the state of Georgia would be a mistake at this time. My basic reasons are listed below.

1. As curator of reptiles at the Okefenokee Park near Waycross, Georgia, I am in an excellent position to state that the eastern indigo snake is no more rare in the state of Georgia than the diamondback rattlesnake (*Crotalus adamanteus*) or any other snake. Therefore, the indigo, first of all, does not qualify as an endangered species.

2. The vast majority of the people of the state of Georgia do not even know what an indigo snake looks like, what he really is, or worse yet, even care a thing about any snake one way or the other. There is not a town in the state of Georgia where people do not brag about the snakes they kill. To educate these people, change their ways, would be all but impossible.

Can We Find a Hiding Place, Too? • 139

3. Every concerned herpetologist in this state recognizes the fact that during the warm months of the year, more snakes, including indigos, are accidentally or intentionally killed by automobiles in one twenty-four-hour period than all the snake hunters combined could capture in this state in a whole year. No law could possibly protect the wild animals from automobiles.
4. The indigo's habitat is restricted to high ground—sand or oak ridges. Most of this type of land belongs to private citizens who have the right to take trees, build dams or lakes, plow new ground, build homes, or anything else they wish to do. In the past three years, and especially the past several months, I have witnessed time and again many prime indigo snake territories absolutely demolished and snakes buried alive as the tracks of bulldozers sealed them underground forever. If a landowner can legally kill hundreds of snakes and be within his rights, why should it be put into law that a person cannot capture them alive and unharmed?
5. At this point we are not sure of the total effect of insecticides on the snake population, but the effect has to be adverse. The endangered species law will not stop landowners from using insecticides to insure their crops.
6. A recent study by Auburn University shows that gasoline kills snakes. Rattlesnake roundups are becoming more popular, and the method of capturing snakes is to gas them in gopher tortoise holes. This kills indigos—maybe by mistake, but how could the endangered species law stop the rattlesnake round-ups?
7. Part of the intent of this law is to stop the sale of indigos. When the state of Florida passed this law for their indigos, the price of an indigo snake tripled almost overnight. If Georgia passes such a law one immediate result will be a higher price yet on "Alabama" and "South Carolina" indigos.

Certain people feel it is wrong to capture any type of snake. As for the indigo, the high price on it means fewer people can afford one, but those that do purchase one tend to take much better care of it—if for no other reason than to protect their investment. A properly taken care of indigo snake thrives well in captivity for years.

The endangered species law would stop none of the real killers of snakes. It would merely make it illegal to capture them alive and unharmed.

The state of Georgia surely recognizes the fact that all our native species deserve some measure of protection. It seems far more feasible, and much less expensive, to utilize as much property presently owned by the state as possible for the full protection and also the proper management of all species of wildlife, including snakes, within its boundaries, and to encourage private citizens, landowners, and lumber companies to do the same.

In beauty and balance,
DICK (OKEFENOKEE JOE) FLOOD
Okefenokee Swamp Park

OJ's letter causes reflection and perhaps dismay. His points penetrate, for the problems relate to all species. (Although my example has been with snakes, all species and environments are in trouble for two reasons: ecological ignorance and cultural attitudes.) The following points must be heeded by all and the resultant questions need to be answered before too long.

1. Frequently we do not know the ecology of a species well enough to make prudent decisions. Are the American people willing to pay the price for full-scale research programs to get the answers?

2. Many people are ignorant of the ecology and life history of most species. How many people will take the time to find out where the critical habitats of a rare species are? Are we willing to pay the taxes needed to support the necessary educational programs?

3. Highway deaths are too high for humans, but the numbers are unspeakable for reptiles, amphibians, and small mammals. Seeing and avoiding animals on the road is a matter of training, preceded by an attitude of caring. Will we accept the cost to instill such concern in the nation's drivers? Should we impose a moratorium on highway construction and even close some that are now open?

4. Owning land is a sacred right in the United States. How can we prevent habitat destruction by landowners, particularly those who see a major economic gain in the offing? Can a system that is compatible environmentally, politically, and economically be worked out under our present form of government and philoso-

Can We Find a Hiding Place, Too? • 141

phy? I am not aware that any of the major environmentalist groups have proposed a plan to change our property ownership laws.

5. What about the agricultural systems? Should the government ban each insecticide *before* use until its environmental effect is thoroughly known and evaluated? I know of no organizations that have effectively promoted this measure.

6. Hunting and fishing by sportsmen take many animal lives each year in the United States. Are they to be challenged when they affect species that are not part of their game plan?

7. Should we establish stricter regulations on the sale and exchange of animals for pets? The costs of present attempts at regulation are mounting. Is taxation an acceptable way to pay for the costs involved in controlling the excesses in the pet industry?

Underlying any potential to change these legal and attitudinal considerations is an undeserved complacency that resides in our society that scientists already know the important basic principles in each field of science. In ecology in particular and biology in general the surface hardly has been broken. We understand only a minor proportion of what is to be known about natural environments and their component plants and animals. Yet this basic foundation, which is so incomplete, is essential to our making prudent judgments about environmental management. Ecologists are beginning to get the message that we have a lot to learn. Society likewise needs to be aware of our problem and accept a responsibility to support ecological research.

We have two serious problems: (1) we do not have the ecological knowledge that we need; and (2) we have a long, long way to go before this country develops an environmental ethic that serves our needs. Recognizing the problems is the first step. And the solutions that are before us may be as unpalatable as the worst medicine we have ever taken. But a big dose may be needed if we are to keep from dying of the disease.

CHAPTER 11

Teaching the Public:

How to Hold an Audience
with a Snake

Snakes are a reliable means of getting someone's attention for whatever reason. Someone giving a talk on the ecology of snakes invariably captures the interest of a class of students by pulling a shiny black kingsnake with bright yellow bands out of a cloth sack. Important businessmen immediately will follow your orders to back away from the guest speaker's table if you use a five-foot canebrake rattlesnake as an example of poisonous snakes of the region. Unfortunately, snakes usually receive the wrong kind of attention, so a well-presented "snake talk" is an opportunity to modify a few people's focus on the issue.

Giving a snake talk to a group of any sort can be a really gratifying experience. Among the best audiences imaginable for such talks have been the groups of DuPont employees at the Savannah River Plant. The Savannah River Ecology Laboratory was somewhat the maverick on the SRP because our forty to sixty students and employees were prone to dress in the manner of college students, whereas DuPont personnel were inclined to dress in the manner of DuPont personnel. Nonetheless, DuPont has the best safety program in industry. And they really work at it. Weekly safety talks to everyone. Signs. Awards. More talks. And pretty soon you run out of interesting topics.

One day a DuPont executive friend of mine, Bill Hale, asked me to give a talk on the safety hazards of poisonous snakes. I did, using live snakes, milking a cottonmouth in the DuPont lab director's personal ashtray, and accidentally dropping a huge rattlesnake on the freshly waxed floor. After an amusing moment of watching the first two rows of folding chairs topple backward with the escape response of the twenty people sitting there, I set about trying to pick up the animal. Every time I pinned its head to the floor and

Hold an Audience with a Snake • 143

started to reach down, the chin would slip on the shiny floor and the head would be out from under the snake stick.

All of the DuPonters were standing now, amid an array of fallen chairs. I tried to look as calm as ever. No rattlesnake could, or would, ever try to catch you in a large room. So I wasn't really scared, except of being embarrassed. I did have an obligation to remove the animal from the doorway where it had finally crawled. The big canebrake rattlesnake liked the doorway, surely not because it held me and fifty-six DuPonters at bay—instead because the indentation of the door probably had a cavelike appearance to which the snake could relate. The snake liked the security and had decided to stay there.

I was getting nervous that before long the DuPonters would think I was helpless in my own field. So far, they thought this scene was part of the show. But time was getting short. I needed to get the rattlesnake back under control. I picked up the large empty snake sack, ready to try anything to get this situation settled. I laid one side of the open end on the floor about six inches from the snake's nose. The long black tongue emerged inquisitively and withdrew. Back and forth it went, searching for chemical clues of what was happening.

Ordinarily, I would not put my hand a foot above a five-foot canebrake rattlesnake, but I was determined to end this mess one way or another. I tapped the black velvet tail, which began to whir. The zinging sound had an instant stilling effect on the captive audience. And then the snake did as I had hoped—crawled forward so that its head went into the back of the bag. I flipped the sack upright, pushing the rear third of the animal on in. As I spun the sack to assure its remaining at the bottom, the applause was a welcome sound above the continuous rattling. I gave about one hundred snake talks over the next four years before the local DuPont management disallowed presentations using live snakes. Too dangerous for a safety talk, the management said. Maybe they were right.

But public talks on snakes or other forms of wildlife by scientists have served greatly in the advance of understanding animals and ecology. Most people have such an acquired fear and ignorance of snakes that any true information they get is an advancement. I say "true" information because of all the false material that even

Snakes, particularly large poisonous ones such as an eastern diamondback rattle-snake, can be used to capture the attention of an audience of any sort. Sometimes even the person giving the talk can be somewhat awed by the presentation.

educated people dish out about snakes. In fact, the subject of snakes represents one of the few about which ignorance is actually taught.

Snake talks can be huge successes or near-disasters because of the live, and sometimes dangerous, props used. A friend of mine told me of a snake talk mishap that was the best attention getter he had ever seen. Bob Shoop was to talk to a troop of Brownies about snakes and he asked a student to come along. Dr. Shoop had noticed the student's enthusiasm on a field trip he had led a few days earlier, as part of a herpetology course he was teaching, and wanted to encourage him. On the way to the Brownie troop meeting, the student even asked if he could do some of the talking. He mentioned that he had brought a few of his own snakes, recently caught, if Dr. Shoop would let him use them. At the

Hold an Audience with a Snake • 145

meeting, in the spirit of promoting the teaching profession and of educating Brownie scouts about why there was no need to fear snakes, Bob actually deferred to the student and introduced him as the one who would give the presentation. Bob sat to one side to watch as the young man began to open the first sack. He had explained to the politely quiet but attentive audience of little girls and anxious mothers that he wanted to hold a snake while he talked, so they could see that there was no reason to be afraid.

Then out it came! The biggest blue racer that Bob had ever seen—not necessarily the meanest blue racer, because every last one of them is mean. But this one was certainly mean enough as it left the confines of the sack and headed straight for the student's face. And then amid such emotions as amazement, astonishment, and horror, the snake latched on to the student's nose.

All racers bite. They're not poisonous, but they do bite, and they don't stop biting. They chew away unmercifully. And so it did, gobbling away at the student's nose with a score of pinpoint-sized teeth that drew more blood than one would imagine would be there. Then, to Bob's further dismay, the student kept talking to his stunned audience as if nothing had happened. Understandably he had everyone's attention as he held a five-foot blue racer by the tail while the other end held his nose. Blood poured over his lips and chin as he explained that racers were harmless. The Brownies were jumping and squealing. The troop leaders and mothers were yelling at them not to look, while at the same time screaming at them to be quiet and that everything was all right. I don't know what else herpetologists taught the public that day, but undoubtedly several people learned not to use a big racer as the lead presentation in a snake talk. Harmless or not.

That actually sums up the situation. Practically anything the public learns about reptiles and amphibians is worthwhile, considering how painfully little is known. Ignorance and the level of actual misinformation about these groups of animals rival that of any other group that is so much a part of our local environments. As indicated in this book, scientists still have a world of information to learn about herpetology. But what the average lay person knows about the subject is almost embarrassing for a country that espouses education and knowledge. We really need to try to do better.

Selected References
in Herpetology

Anyone interested in pursuing the field of herpetology in depth has an array of books and journals from which to select. Some of the publications are more technically oriented than others but any of the following will offer some enlightenment to lay people interested in learning more about reptiles and amphibians.

Technical Journals in Herpetology

Several professional journals are devoted exclusively to herpetology. In the United States two professional societies, the Herpetologists' League (HL) and the Society for the Study of Reptiles and Amphibians (SSAR), publish herpetological journals. The American Society of Ichthyologists and Herpetologists (ASIH) also publishes a journal of which half of the articles are herpetological studies. Herpetological journals of the world, and the societies which they represent, include the following:

Amphibia—Reptilia (Societas Europaea Herpetologica)
Australian Journal of Herpetology (Australian Herpetologists' League)
British Journal of Herpetology (British Herpetological Society)
Copeia (ASIH)
Herpetofauna (Australasian Affiliation of Herpetological Societies)
Herpetologica (HL)
Herpetological Review (SSAR)
Japanese Journal of Herpetology (Herpetological Society of Japan)
Journal of Herpetology (SSAR)
Salamandra (Deutschen gesellschaft für Herpetologie und Terrarienkunde)
Snake (Japan Snake Institute)

State and Regional Field Books on Reptiles and Amphibians of the United States and Canada

Field books are useful to anyone interested in identifying the reptiles and amphibians of an area and in learning something of their habits and ecology. Such books vary widely in quality and usefulness and may be confined to a geographic region or restricted to a particular taxonomic group. A few examples are listed.

Eastern United States

Conant, Roger. 1975. *A Field Guide to Reptiles and Amphibians of Eastern and Central North America*. Boston: Houghton Mifflin Co.

Martof, Bernard S., William M. Palmer, Joseph R. Bailey, and Julian R. Harrison III. 1980. *Amphibians and Reptiles of the Carolinas and Virginia*. Chapel Hill: University of North Carolina Press.

Mount, Robert H. 1975. *The Reptiles and Amphibians of Alabama*. Auburn, Ala.: Auburn University Agricultural Experiment Station.*

Smith, Philip W. 1961. *The Amphibians and Reptiles of Illinois*. Illinois Natural History Survey Bulletin, vol. 28, art. 1.*

Western United States

Stebbins, Robert C. 1966. *A Field Guide to Western Reptiles and Amphibians*. Boston: Houghton Mifflin Co.

Hawaii

McKeown, Sean. 1978. *Hawaiian Reptiles and Amphibians*. Honolulu: Oriental Publishing Co.

Canada and Alaska

Froom, Barbara. 1972. *The Snakes of Canada*. Toronto: McClelland and Stewart.

---

*State accounts of reptiles and/or amphibians have been done for many of the states; the two by Mount and Smith cover most of the species that are found in the eastern United States.

_____. 1976. *The Turtles of Canada*. Toronto: McClelland and Stewart.

Logier, E. B. S. and G. C. Toner. 1961. *Checklist of the Amphibians and Reptiles of Canada and Alaska*. Toronto: Royal Ontario Museum.

Selected Taxonomic Groups in North America

Bishop, Sherman C. 1947. *Handbook of Salamanders: The Salamanders of the United States, of Canada, and of Lower California*. Ithaca, N.Y.: Comstock Publishing Co.

Carr, Archie. 1952. *Handbook of Turtles: The Turtles of the United States, Canada, and Baja California*. Ithaca, N.Y.: Cornell University Press.

Ditmars, R. L. 1951. *Snakes of the World*. New York: Macmillan Co.

Ernst, Carl H. and Roger W. Barbour. 1972. *Turtles of the United States*. Lexington: University Press of Kentucky.

Leviton, Arthur E. 1972. *Reptiles and Amphibians of North America*. New York: Doubleday Publishing Co.

Schmidt, Karl P. and D. Dwight Davis. 1941. *Field Book of Snakes of the United States and Canada*. New York: G. P. Putnam's Sons.

Smith, Hobart M. 1946. *Handbook of Lizards: Lizards of the United States and Canada*. Ithaca, N.Y.: Comstock Publishing Co.

_____. 1978. *Amphibians of North America*. Racine, Wis.: Western Publishing Co.

_____ and Edmund D. Brodie, Jr. 1982. *Reptiles of North America*. Racine, Wis.: Western Publishing Co.

Wright, Albert H. and Anna A. Wright. 1949. *Handbook of Frogs and Toads of the United States and Canada*. Ithaca, N.Y.: Comstock Publishing Co.

_____. 1957. *Handbook of Snakes of the United States and Canada*. Vols. 1 and 2. Ithaca, N.Y.: Cornell University Press.

Textbooks in Herpetology

Two books currently are available for use in advanced undergraduate or graduate level courses in herpetology.

Goin, Coleman J., Olive B. Goin, and George R. Zug. 1978. *Introduction to Herpetology*. San Francisco: W. H. Freeman and Co.

Porter, Kenneth R. 1972. *Herpetology*. Philadelphia: W. B. Saunders Co.

General Works in Herpetology

Many accounts have been written of particular groups of reptiles and amphibians. Some are of a technical nature but many are written for the layman or have portions that are suitable for general reading. A few examples are indicated.

Bellairs, Angus. 1970. *The Life of Reptiles*. Vols. 1 and 2. New York: Universe Books.

Blair, W. Frank. 1960. *The Rusty Lizard, A Population Study*. Austin: University of Texas Press.

Cochran, Doris M. 1961. *Living Amphibians of the World*. Garden City, N.Y.: Doubleday and Co.

Gans, Carl. 1975. *Reptiles of the World*. New York: Ridge Press.

Klauber, Laurence M. 1972. *Rattlesnakes: Their Habits, Life Histories, and Influence on Mankind*. Vols. 1 and 2. Los Angeles: University of California Press.

Lanworn, R. A. 1972. *The Book of Reptiles*. London: Hamlyn Publishing Group.

Minton, Sherman A., Jr., Herndon G. Dowling, and Findlay E. Russell. 1965. *Poisonous Snakes of the World*. Washington, D.C.: Department of the Navy, Bureau of Medicine and Surgery, U.S. Government Printing Office.

Minton, Sherman A., Jr., and Madge R. Minton. 1969. *Venomous Reptiles*. New York: Charles Scribner's Sons.

Neill, Wilfred T. 1971. *Last of the Ruling Reptiles*. New York: Columbia University Press.

Noble, G. Kingsley. 1931. *The Biology of the Amphibia*. New York: McGraw-Hill Book Co. Reprinted 1954, Dover Publications.

Oliver, James. 1955. *The Natural History of Amphibians and Reptiles of North America*. Princeton, N.J.: D. Van Nostrand Co.

Parker, H. W. and Alice G. C. Grandison. 1977. *Snakes—A Natural History*. Ithaca, N.Y.: Cornell University Press.

Pope, Clifford H. 1974. *The Reptile World. A Natural History of the Snakes, Lizards, Turtles, and Crocodilians*. New York: Alfred A. Knopf.

———. 1961. *The Giant Snakes*. London: Routledge and Kegan Paul.

Pritchard, Peter C. H. 1967. *Living Turtles of the World*. Neptune City, N.J.: TFH Publications.

———. 1979. *Encyclopedia of Turtles*. Neptune City, N.J.: TFH Publications.

Schmidt, Karl P. and Robert F. Inger. 1957. *Living Reptiles of the World*. Garden City, N.Y.: Doubleday and Co.

Taylor, Edward H. 1968. *The Caecilians of the World*. Lawrence: University of Kansas Press.

Tinkle, Donald W. 1967. *The Life and Demography of the Side-blotched Lizard, Uta stansburiana*. Miscellaneous Publications of the Museum of Zoology no. 132, pp. 1–182. Ann Arbor: University of Michigan.

Twitty, Victor C. 1966. *Of Scientists and Salamanders*. San Francisco: W. H. Freeman and Co.

World Herpetology—Regional Accounts

Most countries and regions of the world have been explored by herpetologists and many have field guides to the identification, behavior, and ecology of the reptiles and amphibians. Some accounts are old and out of print but remain as the most useful guide to the herpetofauna of a region. The following list is not exhaustive but indicates some of the accounts that would be useful in particular regions outside of North America.

Central and South America

Duellman, William E. 1970. *Hylid Frogs of Middle America*. Vols. 1 and 2. Monograph no. 1. University of Kansas: Museum of Natural History.

———. 1979. *The South American Herpetofauna: Its Origin, Evolution, and Dispersal*. Monograph no. 7. University of Kansas: Museum of Natural History.

Brazil

Amaral, A. 1977. *Serpentes do Brasil: Iconografia Colorida*. Universidade de São Paulo, Brasilia: Instituto Nacional do Livre.

Vanzolini, P. E., Ana Maria M. Ramos-Costa, and Laurie J. Vitt. 1980. *Repteis das Caatingas*. Rio de Janeiro: Academia Brasileira de Ciencias.

Chile

Donoso-Barros, Roberto. 1966. *Reptiles de Chile*. Santiago: University of Chile.

Colombia

Cochran, Doris M. and Coleman J. Goin. 1970. *Frogs of Colombia*. Washington, D.C.: Smithsonian Institution Press.

Costa Rica

Taylor, Edward H. 1951. "A Brief Review of the Snakes of Costa Rica." *Kansas University Science Bulletin* 34(1):3–188.
————. 1954. "Further Studies on the Serpents of Costa Rica." *Kansas University Science Bulletin* 36:673–801.
————. 1956. "A Review of the Lizards of Costa Rica." *Kansas University Science Bulletin* 38:1–322.

Cuba

Barbour, Thomas and C. T. Ramsden. 1919. "The Herpetology of Cuba." Memoirs of the Museum of Comparative Zoology, Harvard. 47:69–214.

Ecuador

Duellman, William E. 1978. *The Biology of an Equatorial Herpetofauna in Amazonian Ecuador*. Museum of Natural History Miscellaneous Publications no. 65, pp. 1–352. Lawrence: University of Kansas.

Guatemala

Stuart, L. C. 1963. *A Checklist of the Herpetofauna of Guatemala*. Miscellaneous Publications of the Museum of Zoology no. 122, pp. 1–150. Ann Arbor: University of Michigan.

Honduras

Meyer, John R. and Larry D. Wilson. 1971. *A Distributional Checklist of the Amphibians of Honduras*. Contributions in Science. Los Angeles: Los Angeles County Museum.

Mexico

Smith, Hobart M. and Rozella B. Smith. 1971–1977. *Synopsis of the Herpetofauna of Mexico*. 6 vols. North Bennington, Vt.: John Johnson.
1971. *Analysis of the Literature on the Mexican Axolotl*. Vol 1.
1973. *Analysis of the Literature Exclusive of the Mexican Axolotl*. Vol. 2.
1976. *Source Analysis and Index for Mexican Reptiles*. Vol. 3.

1976. *Source Analysis and Index for Mexican Amphibians*. Vol. 4.

1977. *Guide to Mexican Amphisbaenians and Crocodilians*. Bibliographic Addendum II. Vol. 5.

1979. *Guide to Mexican Turtles*. Bibliographic Addendum III. Vol. 6.

_____. 1976. *Synopsis of the Herpetofauna of Mexico*. North Bennington, Vt.: John Johnson.

Peru

Dixon, James R. and P. Soini. 1975. *The Reptiles of the Upper Amazon Basin, Iquitos Region, Peru*. I. *Lizards and Amphisbaenians*. Contributions in Biology and Geology. Vol. 4, pp. 1–58. Milwaukee: Milwaukee Public Museum.

_____. 1976. *The Reptiles of the Upper Amazon Basin, Iquitos Region, Peru*. II. *Crocodilians, Turtles and Snakes*. Contributions in Biology and Geology. Vol. 12, pp. 1–91. Milwaukee: Milwaukee Public Museum.

West Indies

Schwartz, Albert and Richard Thomas. 1975. *A Check-list of West Indian Amphibians and Reptiles*. Special Publication. Pittsburgh: Carnegie Museum of Natural History.

Europe

Arnold, E. N. and J. A. Burton. 1978. *A Field Guide to the Reptiles and Amphibians of Britain and Europe*. London: Collins.

Hellmich, W. 1962. *Reptiles and Amphibians of Europe*. London: Blandford Press.

Mertens, R. and H. Wermuth. 1960. *Die Amphibien und Reptilien Europas*. Frankfort: Waldeman Kramer.

Street, Donald. 1979. *The Reptiles of Northern and Central Europe*. London: B. T. Batsford.

England

Smith, Malcomb A. 1964. *The British Amphibians and Reptiles*. London: Collins.

France

Rollinat, R. 1934. *La Vie des Reptiles de la France Centrale*. Paris: Librairie Delagrame.

Russia

Nilol'skii, A. M. 1915–1918 (original); 1962–1964 (translation). *Fauna of Russia and Adjacent Countries*. Jerusalem: Israel Program for Scientific Translation.
1962. Amphibians.
1963. Reptiles. Vol. I. Chelonia and Sauria.
1964. Vol. 2. Reptiles.

Asia

Ceylon

Wall, F. 1921. *Snakes of Ceylon*. Colombo: H. R. Cottle.

China

Liu, C. C. 1950. *The Amphibians of Western China*. Chicago: Natural History Museum Press.
Mao, S. H. and B. Y. Chen. 1980. *Sea Snakes of Taiwan*. Special Publication no. 4. T'aipei, Taiwan: National Science Council.
Pope, Clifford H. 1935. *Natural History of Central Asia*. Vol. 10, *The Reptiles of China*. New York: American Museum of Natural History.

India

Smith, Malcomb A. 1931–1943. *The Fauna of British India. Reptilia and Amphibia*. Vols. 1–3. London: Taylor and Francis.
Wall, F. 1918. "A Popular Treatise on the Common Indian Snakes." Part 24. *Journal of the Bombay Natural History Society* 25:375–82.
Whitaker, Romulus. 1978. *Common Indian Snakes. A Field Guide*. New Delhi: Macmillan Co. of India.

Iran

Anderson, S. C. 1963. "Amphibians and Reptiles from Iran." *Proceedings of the California Academy of Science* 31:417–98.

Iraq

Kahalaf, Kamel T. 1959. *Reptiles of Iraq with Some Notes on the Amphibians*. Baghdad: Ar-Rabitta Press.

Nepal

Swan, L. W. and Arthur E. Leviton. 1962. "The Herpetology of Nepal." *Proceedings of the California Academy of Science* 32:103–47.

Pakistan

Minton, Sherman A., Jr. 1966. "A Contribution to the Herpetology of West Pakistan." *Bulletin of the American Museum of Natural History* 132(2):31–184.

Thailand

Taylor, Edward H. 1965. "The Serpents of Thailand and Adjacent Waters." *Kansas University Science Bulletin* 45:609–1096.

Vietnam

Campden-Main, Simon M. 1970. *A Field Guide to the Snakes of South Vietnam*. Washington, D.C.: U.S. Natural History Museum, Division of Reptiles and Amphibians.

Africa

East Africa

Loveridge, Arthur. 1957. "Checklist of the Reptiles and Amphibians of East Africa (Uganda; Kenya; Tanganyika; Zanzibar)." *Bulletin of the Museum of Comparative Zoology* (Harvard), 117:153–362.

Egypt

Marx, Hymen. 1968. *Checklist of the Reptiles and Amphibians of Egypt*. Special Publication of U.S. Naval Medical Research Unit No. 3 (Cairo).

Malawi

Stewart, Margaret M. 1967. *Amphibians of Malawi*. Albany: State University of New York Press.

Rhodesia

Broadley, Donald G. and E. V. Cock. 1975. *Snakes of Rhodesia*. Salisbury: Langman Rhodesia.

South Africa

FitzSimons, V. F. 1943. *The Lizards of South Africa*. Transvaal Museum Memoirs no. 1, pp. 1–528.

Visser, John. 1979. *Common Snakes of South Africa*. Cape Town: Purnell.

Uganda

Pitman, C. R. S. 1974. *A Guide to the Snakes of Uganda*. Revised edition. London: Wheldon and Wesley.

West Africa

Cansdale, George. 1955. *Reptiles of West Africa*. London: Penguin Books.

Zambia

Broadley, Donald G. 1971. "The Reptiles and Amphibians of Zambia." *Puku. Occasional Papers of the Department of Game and Fish of Zambia* 6:1–143.

Australasia, Indonesia, and Japan

Loveridge, Arthur. 1946. *Reptiles of the Pacific World*. New York: Macmillan Co. Reprinted 1974. Facsimile Reprints in Herpetology. Ohio University, Athens: Society for the Study of Amphibians and Reptiles.

Australia

Cogger, Harold G. 1975. *Reptiles and Amphibians of Australia*. Sydney: A. H. and A. W. Reed.

Kinghorn, J. R. 1964. *The Snakes of Australia*. Sydney: Angus and Robertson.

Worrell, E. 1963. *Reptiles of Australia*. Sydney: Angus and Robertson.

Borneo

Lloyd, Monte, Robert F. Inger, and F. Wayne King. 1968. "On the Diversity of Reptile and Amphibian Species in a Bornean Rain Forest." *American Naturalist* 102:497–515.

Indo-Australian Region

Rooij, N. de. 1917. *The Reptiles of the Indo-Australian Archipelago.* II. *Ophidia.* Leiden, Netherlands: E. J. Brill.

Japan

Stejneger, Leonard. 1907. "Herpetology of Japan and Adjacent Territory." *Bulletin of the United States Natural History Museum* 58:1–577.

Java

Kopstein, F. 1938. "Ein Beitreg zur Eierkunde und zur Fort-pflanzung der Malaiischen Reptilian." *Bulletin of the Raffles Museum,* no. 14.

Malaysia

Berry, P. Y. 1975. *The Amphibian Fauna of Peninsular Malaysia.* Kuala Lumpur: Tropical Press.

New Zealand

Robb, J. 1973. "Reptiles and Amphibia." In *The Natural History of New Zealand.* Wellington: Reed Publishing Co.

Index

Moccasin. *See* Cottonmouth moccasin
Monitor lizards (*Varanus*), 42, 78
Mount, Robert, 86
Murphy, Pat, 12
Murphy, Tom, 114, 126

New Guinea, 42
New Jersey pine barrens, 100
New Orleans, 12
New York, 91
New Zealand, 83
Newt, 90
  European (*Triturus*), 91
  Red-spotted (*Notophthalmus viride-scens*), 89
  Rough-skinned (*Taricha granulosa*), 90
Noosing, 81, 82
North Carolina, 15, 65, 87

Ocotee, South Carolina, 26
Ohio State University, 85
Okefenokee Joe, 138, 139, 141
Okefenokee Swamp Park, 138, 141
Oklahoma, 12, 25
Olympic Mountains, 101
Oregon, 91

Parmenter, Bob, 12, 13, 129, 130
Par Pond, 49, 51, 52, 53, 125, 127, 135, 136
Pascagoula River, 39
Patterson, Karen, 116
Pearl River, 39, 40, 41
Phaeognathus hubrichti, 84, 85, 86
Pitfall trap, 112, 113, 117, 119
Pit viper, 7, 20, 23, 28, 30, 33, 34
Plummer, Michael, 125
Poaching, 65, 70
Poison apparatus, 27
Poison injection, 34
Poison sac, 32
Poison gland, 18, 33
Poisonous lizard, 77
Poisonous stinger, 35
Polychrus lizard, 77
Pond C, 50
Python, 18, 32, 36, 41

Queen snake (*Regina septemvittata*), 25, 26

Racer (*Coluber constrictor*), 21, 35, 146; black, 20; blue, 146
Racerunner, Six-lined (*Cnemidophorus sexlineatus*), 2, 80
Radioactive tagging technique, 119, 120, 122, 124
Radiotelemetry, 122, 124, 126, 127
Rainbow Bay, 116
Rattlesnake, 27, 28, 30, 31, 33, 35, 111, 143, 173; gassing burrows of, 111; meat of, 12; roundups, 12, 25, 111, 140
  Canebrake (*Crotalus horridus*), 5, 6, 7, 12, 28, 137, 143, 144
  Eastern diamondback (*Crotalus adamanteus*), 25, 28, 30, 111, 138, 139, 145
  Massasauga (*Sistrurus catenatus*), 30
  Pygmy (*Sistrurus miliarius*), 30
  Sidewinder (*Crotalus cerastes*), 32
  Timber (*Crotalus horridus*), 28, 30
  Western diamondback (*Crotalus atrox*), 73
Road collecting, 110, 111

Salamander, 84–95; size of, 88, 89; larvae of, 91, 92; cannibalism of, 91, 92; blind species, 92. *See also* Newt
  Congo eel (*Amphiuma means*), 88
  Dwarf (*Eurycea quadridigitata*), 88, 92
  Georgia blind (*Haideotriton wallacei*), 92
  Greater siren (*Siren lacertina*), 89
  Hellbender (*Cryptobranchus alleganiensis*), 18, 88
  Marbled (*Ambystoma opacum*), 89
  Mole (*Ambystomatidae*), 12, 90, 116, 124
  Red hills (*Phaeognathus hubrichti*), 86, 87
  Red (*Pseudotriton ruber*), 90
  Siren (*Siren*), 88, 89
  Spring lizard, 91
  Texas blind (*Typhlomolge rathbuni*), 92
  Tiger (*Ambystoma tigrinum*), 91
  Two-lined (*Eurycea bislineata*), 90
  Woodland (*Plethodon*), 88
Salmonella, 14
Savannah River, 97, 105, 106, 107
Savannah River Ecology Laboratory

Index • 163